THE
CASTLE

A NOVEL SET IN CORNWALL DURING
THE ENGLISH CIVIL WAR

BY

MARK KILBURN

Published by borderlandpublishing
ISBN: 9798862561159

For Annie, who lived near the castle.

CONTENTS

1.

(i)

Elowen stood motionless in the long grass, nestled between the oaks, heather, and burdock, looking out onto a lifeless winding road. It was the hour after dawn, when low-lying mists sweep across fields and smoke begins to rise from the isolated dwellings hidden around the forest's edge. A boy scuttled beside her – Maben, the mute, touched by the moon. Unsure as to why Elowen had stopped, he fidgeted with a piece of dry wood and mumbled in that strange manner of his, a sound that was not language but the remnants of something, a long-forgotten ritual perhaps. Whatever it was, Elowen ordered him quiet and pulled tight the slingshot tied around her waist. Beyond the road lay more woodland – a fresh, dark estate, teeming with life at this hour. It was there she would lay traps and fill the sack that the mute boy carried with fresh meat. But she remained still, gauging the air, alert to the shifting rhythms of the new day. For, in the far distance, she heard a rumbling sound, a sound that was gathering beneath the earth like thunder.

Maben squatted. Thunder frightened him. Elowen knelt and made him cover his ears. She knew all about the boy's anxieties, the tics and nightmares that governed his life. He preferred the peace of the forest, the coolness of air. As the thunder drew closer, Maben curled himself into a muscle-tight ball, as if he was imprisoned in a space governed by fear.

Six horses pulling a carriage surged round the bend – black and sleek and fierce as they ran into the straight. Two drivers sat out front wearing long grey coats buttoned at the neck; a footman of robust size stood on a platform at the rear. Such a sight, early in morning, inspired tales of ghosts and supernatural beings. It set Elowen to thinking: *inside this carriage sits either the devil or the king of England.*

The carriage roared along the road, a road that led to Falmouth town. As it advanced, the maul of horses' hooves gave way to a high-pitched squeal, a grinding sound that Elowen had never before heard. The two drivers yelled, pulled hard on the reins. The horses reared and whinnied, nostrils wide, eyes distending. The carriage swerved this way and that and, for a moment, it seemed that it would tip onto its side and come to an unfortunate end. Suddenly Elowen realised what had happened: an axle had buckled, shifting the weight. But the drivers used every fibre to pull the beasts steady, and the carriage slowed enough to right itself, coming to a halt in a cloud of dust not far from where the young hunters hid.

As the atmosphere settled, Elowen stroked Maben's head, soothing his anxieties, preventing him from calling out. She saw that the colour of the carriage matched the horses – jet black with three white feathers painted on the side door. As the plumes of dust began to clear, Maben shifted in the long grass.

'Be still!' Elowen whispered. 'They must not see us. We are folk who should have no knowledge of these things.'

She watched as the two drivers leapt from their seats to examine the broken rear wheel. Elowen heard hammering, heaving, and shouts of, 'This way, damn you!' and 'Push, I say – push, push, and push again!' The large footman who stood at the rear climbed down from his tailboard and walked to the side carriage door. A broad bull-like man with a grey beard and ponytail, Elowen caught him well in her sight. She watched as he gently opened the carriage door, bowed, took off his greatcoat, and laid it on the ground.

Elowen gasped as she saw a slender figure climb out – a young man with long, curling, lacquered hair. He was wearing the finest clothes: a black embroidered jacket, silk breeches and high buckled shoes. His felt hat, marked with a red plume, brushed the top of the carriage door as he alighted onto the footman's coat. Then, in a graceful pose, he stood for a while and took in the scenery. The footman bowed again and, as if in expectation of robbers or cut throats, took up a defensive position at a refined distance to the rear of the carriage where he could best observe and prevent other interruptions to this most important of travellers.

The drivers continued to heave and push but the wheel, it seemed, could not be fixed. The longer they laboured, the more Elowen sensed danger. She unburdened herself of a number of stones from the pocket of her sheepskin, piling them within reach.

'It will soon be over, Maben,' she whispered. 'We must wait until these men are set on their way.'

After a while, the younger man in the fine clothes grew impatient. He summoned the footman who gave another low bow before receiving his orders. Then, after a discussion with the drivers, the footman loosened three of the horses from the main harness. Using saddles stored in the rear section of the carriage, the drivers helped prepare the horses for riding whereupon the young male traveller was helped into a mounted position by the broad footman and eased into the saddle. With the two drivers riding either side of the younger man, and with the carriage left in a state of disrepair, the three continued their journey in the direction of Falmouth town, leaving the footman alone.

A quietness descended. Elowen wondered why the footman had been left behind. It soon became clear: there was work for him to do. First, he carried a chest from the carriage and left it at a distance before returning for a short-handled shovel. He began, with great purpose, to dig a hole a good number of yards away from where the carriage sat. It took him a short hour. Elowen watched intently as he set the chest in its grave, covering it well with earth, stones and grass. When the job was done, he clapped his hands in satisfied appreciation, then eased his broad frame onto a small stool he recovered from the carriage's rear. The footman sat at rest for a while. He seemed in no hurry. Elowen considered that he was waiting for the drivers' return.

Maben began to whine. Elowen snapped in his ear: 'Quiet, boy! Do you want us to hang?' It proved the wrong thing to say. The boy screamed, a high, piercing rasp, loud enough for the drowsy footman of robust size to take note.

Elowen watched; the brute was marking their direction. He stood and recovered his greatcoat, brushing it down before easing his thick arms and barrel chest into it, buttoning the top collar.

'Who's there!' he bellowed. 'In the name of the king – stand and be seen!'

Elowen ducked, lay herself flat in the long grass.

'Quiet, Maben.' Surely now, she thought, the footman was climbing the hillock, like an angry bullock that had picked up an enticing scent. She raised her head, peered once more over the tips of the long grass, saw the man within distance of where they lay. Elowen gasped: he was carrying a musket, primed for good use.

'Maben – we must turn and run into the forest,' she said. But her words, in the tumult of the boy's fear, were lost. He screamed once more.

'Show yourselves, rabbits!' the footman shouted. 'I'll be quick and clean in my killing.'

Elowen could hear the man close by, his great feet grinding the fresh young grass. If they ran, he would dispatch them both with a single shot.

'Show yourselves and let's be done with it!' he wheezed.

Elowen took up one of the stones and untied her slingshot from her waist. She measured her breath and stood, quick and confident, causing the footman to halt and take in the creature he was hunting. The size of her made him smile.

'A bunny!' he chuckled and lifted his musket into a shooting position, the powder sweet and dry between his finger and thumb, the cord and match hanging ready about his neck. Elowen set the stone in its cradle, whispered an incantation that asked for her slingshot to see her well. She whipped the coiled leather three times above her head before unleashing her ammunition with all her might. The stone travelled straight and true, quenching the air as it whistled at great speed. The footman's eyes bulged as he realised his fate. With a smitch of sound, Elowen's stone landed full square in the centre of the footman's forehead before dropping to the ground with a dainty thud. The man stood for a moment as if a spectre had crossed his path, the shock waves of impact travelling deep within his skull. Then he crumpled and fell backwards into the long grass where he lay without so much as a twitch of movement, seemingly at rest.

(ii)

Elowen and Maben stood over the footman's body. His eyes were open and the centre of his forehead, where the stone struck, had left a soft depression in the skin. Elowen wondered if he was pretending to be dead. As the thought took hold, she became fearful that he might rise up without warning and snap both their necks. Cautiously she reached down and took up the musket, aimed it at his head a while and ordered Maben to kick the legs several times before concluding that yes, the monster had indeed breathed his last.

They each took hold of one of the footman's ankles and tried to drag the body into the woods, managing only a few inches before deciding it was too heavy. Elowen, lacking coin, placed stones on the dead man's eyes before telling Maben to collect branches and leaves. They would throw as much over him as they could, preferably until the mighty fellow disappeared from plain sight. The boy did as he was told, scampering into the forest a number of times, dumping wood and foliage beside Elowen who carefully covered the corpse. When it was done, she considered saying a prayer but knew none. Instead, she pushed the footman's musket into the pyre to rest alongside him. She told Maben to stay and keep watch.

Elowen made her way down the hillock to the abandoned carriage. She gasped when she looked inside. *Such luxury!* The inside of the carriage looked like a fancy house. A red velvet seat was imprinted with the three white feathers; black velvet curtains were available to shade the windows; an array of liquid victuals, contained in cut glass decanters, sat snug in a red velvet cabinet, each glass item depressed within its own holder. Elowen considered pulling the plush velvet buttoned seat out and keeping it for herself. But the task was too great. What's more, time was against her; she knew the drivers would soon return.

She moved beyond the carriage to the spot where the footman had been digging. He had done a good job because Elowen had to brush the earth several times to identify the contours of the rectangular hole. When it revealed itself, she clawed away the soft earth, then began raking the soil to uncover the thing hidden. It took only a few minutes to reveal a buried chest – five hands in length, four hands in width. It was locked, as she expected, which made Elowen even more eager to investigate its contents. Three feathers were carved on the lid as well as some Latin text enclosed within a carved scroll that she did not understand. The weight of the thing surprised her. With a supreme effort, her fingers tight around the brass side handle, Elowen lifted the chest out from its grave. Numerous objects clunked and clattered within. She ran to the rear of the carriage and called out:

'Maben! Maben! Come now!'

When there was no answer or sight of the boy, she was made aware of the three remaining horses shifting to and fro. The animals were murmuring as if they had been unsettled.

'Maben? Maben? Where are you, boy?'

He was stroking the bent head of one of them, his cheek pressed firmly above the great black's mouth. And he was whispering into its ear, those strange contortions of language that no human could understand.

'Maben – we must leave!'

There was no response. Elowen had never seen the boy so calm, so content. Maben was shy and not given to affection, even toward Ann and Bethsany, his wards. It was said he had been one of two babes left on the porch of a church and mistress Ann had vowed, along with Bethsany her sister, to care for the boy. Even when the child revealed he was lacking in wits, Ann and Bethsany resolved to stand by him, teaching him as best they could to eat with good manners and mumble his prayers at night. Maben remained a strange, lonely child, wary of folk. How different he was now, Elowen thought, as he patted each animal, showing hitherto unrealised devotion.

'Maben!' Elowen walked up to him, tried to guide him away from the towering beasts. 'If the drivers return, we will be hanged. You must help me carry the chest into the wood.'

Reluctantly he obeyed. She fed her slingshot through the chest's handle and together they pulled the thing like a sledge to the brow of the hillock, past the body of the footman, until they crossed the threshold of the forest and were able to rest. Elowen could see the boy's unhappiness, felt his childish yearning to feel the warmth of the three black horses. And so she made a decision that she knew was both dangerous and reckless.

'Come,' she said. 'We must work quickly. Hurry, boy.'

They ran towards the carriage, frightened that at any moment the two drivers would reappear accompanied by soldiers from the castle.

'The horses!' she shouted. 'Free them from their harness.'

They each took on a role. Old Elijah, their forest neighbour, had taught Elowen how to dress a horse. She unthreaded the leather fastenings and looped them under the horses' bellies. The harness that held them was of the finest quality – thick black leather, polished silver bits, and pretty brass clasps. She noticed that the thicker parts of the harness had been branded with the sign of the three feathers. What did it mean? she wondered.

The animals' excitement began to rise as they realised they were being untethered. Maben calmed them. When Elowen had lifted the final strap, she threw the harness to one side.

'Now, boy – send them on their way.'

At first it seemed that he didn't understand what she meant. Then his face transformed itself into a vision of glee. He smacked the rump of the first horse. It raised itself onto its hind legs and bolted across the grasslands, causing Maben to whoop with joy. There was no need for him to encourage the other two horses – they quickly followed their leader. Maben continued to whoop and jump and wave to the three animals as they galloped free into the far distance.

Then Elowen once again gauged the taut, changeable atmosphere of the day.

'Quiet,' she said, lifting her head. Riders were approaching.

2.

(i)

Before the soldiers from the castle arrived to gaze upon the stricken carriage, Elowen and Maben dragged the chest further into the forest and began to dig a fresh grave. Elowen had taken the footman's short shovel and they worked silently and methodically until both items were safely underground. They heard shouts from the road, as well as the hammering of iron. Elowen knew full well that if the soldiers discovered the footman's body their crime would be found out. But it seemed that another course of thinking had taken hold. As she once again covered the chest with earth, she heard angry shouts that the footman was to blame. The soldiers, it seemed, believed that he had made off by himself. And it was he, they said, as they stared into the empty hole, who was in possession of the royal chest. Without spare horses to harness the carriage, the soldiers left the scene, bound for Pendennis Castle to impart their unfavourable news.

As the sky turned grey and light rain began to fall in a misty haze, Elowen and Maben revealed themselves from their hiding place and moved among the trees they knew so well. A cold dampness enveloped them, settling in their hair, their clothes, inside their thin, leather boots. They did not

11

speak as they walked, each content in the presence of the other, aware that even now the king's soldiers at Pendennis were mustering to search for a traitor who, unbeknown to them, was lying with his musket beneath a mound of wood and leaves. Elowen looked up, tasted the rain. It was as if the actions of that morning had charged the air with possibility, settling on the cusp of a secret that was about to be revealed.

After a while, Elowen began to walk with her usual swagger, clearing an invisible pathway with a long stick. She was a slender girl of sixteen summers with brown shoulder-length hair and piercing grey eyes. She possessed a harsh uncompromising face that reflected her harsh uncompromising life – a life lived on the grasslands high above the town. The thick brown sheepskin jacket that she wore, armless and belted with her slingshot, made her body look fuller than it was – a useful deception which served her well. She could hunt and fight as well as any boy her age. Her temper was even, though never to be underestimated.

Elowen's animal traps were scattered over a wide area, hidden amongst thick bramble, identified by markers only she knew. Rabbits were her prey, as well as squirrels and the occasional bird – small things that would sit well in her grandmother's cooking pot.

She took a rough cloth from the pocket of her coat and wiped her face. Even in the wet she felt at home in this pungent place. The trees were endowed with mystic properties: the great oaks had been worshipped at harvest-time by the ancients; the hazel offered all good people wisdom; the yew was the tree of death, its wood helping to guide lost souls to their resting place. Elowen's grandmother, who followed the old ways, had taught her about such things. Ever since Elowen was a child, the old woman had encouraged faith in the mysteries, much to the dismay of their God-fearing neighbour, Ann Netherton. In the town, Elowen's grandmother had been marked as a witch which was why she was content to live on the edge of the forest, a place of solitude and mystery where many feared to tread.

Elowen stopped. At the sight of an elm, she raised her hand in benediction, as if she were reaching beyond the canopy of leaves to the sky above. What, she wondered, would her grandmother say if she learned that her granddaughter had killed one of the king's footmen?

Maben, following at a pace behind, watched his friend. He began to snigger but returned to silence as a rustling among the leaves caught them unawares. A moment of caution lingered, then passed, as a sprightly vixen emerged, galloping towards the furze.

'Come,' said the girl. 'Let us move forward without fear, away from all we have witnessed.'

Maben surged ahead. Thin, pale, with thick fair hair as dry as barnyard hay, his movements were unconstrained. He skipped and jumped as if a demonic tic lurked deep inside him. He swooped and picked up a dry cone, examined it, threw it with the same, then kicked a piece of lichen bark, crouching to see the insects squirm before his gaze. Being the younger of the two, he followed Elowen in keen adoration, observing her as she moved through the forest, entranced as she knelt by a marker and exposed a well-covered trap to the light.

A nervous twitch of grey fur, then sudden movement.

Weightier than she expected, Elowen lifted the trap door and reached in, pulling out a startled rabbit by its neck. She held it in the mulch before dispatching it with a clean twist of her wrists. She bound the paws and rear legs, then eased the still pliant carcass into the small sack.

'Here,' she said.

Maben took hold, peeked inside, sniffed the kill, then held the sack tight against his belly, as if endeavouring once more to perform a long-forgotten ritual.

A strange boy indeed, thought Elowen. *Touched by the moon. Let him find pleasure where he can.*

She moved on with a feeling of contentment now that the forest had given up the first of its offerings. Her grandmother would be pleased – nothing would go to waste. The blood, offal, trimmings – all would be consumed. The pelt fashioned into a hat to sell, the feet sold as amulets. Even the bones would be washed then arranged in a peculiar fashion for market – a rattle chime to scare birds from a vegetable patch, perhaps, or else ground to a powder and mixed with daub to strengthen a neighbour's wall.

Within the hour their bounty had increased: a second rabbit, a pigeon, a squirrel added to the sack. Maben slung the sack over his shoulder and walked with a long stick of his own, imitating Elowen's actions – solid, sweeping movements from left to right in a show of mastery and completeness.

The rain stopped; the swirling grey clouds began to pass. Home was their destination. And yet Elowen knew that the forest was a place of surprise, always eager to throw up new obstacles on a whim.

As they were about to emerge into the open grasslands, Elowen came to a halt. She crouched down, placed a finger to her lips. Through the trees she could see two horses tethered beside a rough wooden shack that lay in a coppice. It was the home of their good neighbour, Old Elijah, one of a number of poor souls who lived in this wilderness. A flash of red accompanied by the harsh rattle of pots and pans told Elowen all she needed to know about Elijah's visitors: the horses belonged to soldiers of the king — soldiers from Pendennis Castle — in search of food, weapons, and honest answers about an abandoned royal carriage.

(ii)

As they waited for the soldiers to depart, Elowen considered whether Maben should be sent home to raise the alarm. She thought of her grandmother, alone in her wooden dwelling, a dwelling that was as ramshackle as Old Elijah's. Maben's home was little better, though it was fashioned out of brick. And Bethsany and Ann, the strange boy's guardians, would fret at the thought of soldiers in their midst. No, thought Elowen — best wait in silence, even though Maben's infernal fidgeting might alert the king's men.

Soon, two soldiers appeared. They took hold of their horses, re-mounted and cantered across the grassy plain. Elowen stood, whispered to Maben that he should advance with caution. Old Elijah's shack — a flimsy structure of wood and daub which had been the old man's home for so many years — remained quiet. A sense of foreboding engulfed the two as they contemplated what they might find.

When they entered, the old man was busy putting things in their rightful place – difficult for someone who had lost half of his leg. His pots and pans had been thrown to the floor, trinkets and cloth scattered about the place. He turned and looked at his young visitors – wild eyed, fearful, then breaking into a wry smile when he acknowledged who had arrived.

'There's nothing for 'em here,' he said. 'Rogue soldiers ha' been known to set a man to fire and worse if 'ee refuses 'em. Puts their tempers up, it does. An' I'm all alone in the world, so's a crime can pass by unnoticed.'

He moved unsteadily around the damp, mildewed single room that was his home. Skinny, with only several long strands of hair sprouting from his crown, Old Elijah was dressed in his usual rags, his half leg wrapped in a filthy piece of hessian. Toothless, his tongue and mouth remained in constant motion, as if his jaw was somehow independent, desperate to free itself from his head.

'Dear Elijah! Did they speak of a carriage?' asked Elowen, not wanting to give too much away. 'We saw one, black as night, travelling in the direction of the castle.'

'No word o' a carriage. Plunder they wuz after, but there's little enough 'ere to tempt 'em into sinfulness.'

'And if they should come again?' Elowen wondered aloud.

Elijah lay a hand on the table to set himself to balance.

'Roundheads'll soon be in the town. Thar's when the wrath o' Satan'll be set upon us. Theyse can hang and burn me here; I's old and nobody'll care for my worn skin. But youse two rats o' the forest – get y'selves far away is my advice. An' take mistress Ann n' Bethsany away too.'

He poured them a cup of cider from a clay flask which lay hidden in the corner, laughing as he did so.

'No sa wise after all, wurse they?' he chuckled.

After they had drunk, Elowen gave up the squirrel from their sack. Old Elijah praised their generosity and said if only soldiers were blessed with the same good nature, then the country would not be at war and tearing itself asunder.

Satisfied that the old man was as comfortable as he could be, Elowen and Maben left Old Elijah's dwelling, his words: 'Beware o' the castle's men! Theyse'll pressgang youse into service! Beware o' Black Tom's men! Theyse'll string youse up for an afternoon's sport!' following them as they went.

(iii)

Elowen was content to amble across the open grasslands. If the soldiers reappeared to pressgang her into service, she would tell them that her grandmother was an old spinster who had no one to protect her. Surely the king and his men would understand? She could not leave the old woman who had raised her from a babe to fend for herself.

Maben ran ahead in that disjointed manner of his. The inlet came into view – the broad waters that flowed from the open sea into the harbour approaches, with its myriad streams and gullies that Elowen had gazed upon all her life. She looked about the open ground and spied some of the rickety dwellings of others who lived in these parts. She knew them all – poor folk scratching the land; folk who stayed away from the town and who were content to avoid authority and live out their simple lives in peace. They were proud, independent people – Cornish people – who valued their own enterprise, wanting nothing they hadn't earned. Apart from her first year on earth, before her mother fled to Cornwall from London, this was the only world Elowen had known – a world that consisted of her grandmother, the forest, the sea and Falmouth town with its marketplace, church, taverns and harbour.

Elowen was aware that times were strange, that the country was at war. Old Elijah had told her as much one day when she called by after checking her traps. The king had fled to Oxford and there was anger and division between Crown and Parliament – a 'great fallin' out' as Elijah called it. Elowen also knew that the 'great falling out' was making its way towards Cornwall. Town after town in the south-west was kneeling to Fairfax's New Model Army. Elowen's grandmother was scared that she would be taken by the Roundheads – forced to don an orange sash and fight against the king. But Elowen tried to calm her fears. The folk who lived in these parts were outliers, tinkers, ne'er-do-wells; folk who were no use to any army. The worst that could happen, Elowen told her, was for a soldier or two to be billeted in their dwelling. And even so, what soldier would stay in these parts? Away from the ale houses, whores, and good meat that could be found in the town? Now she would have to tell her grandmother what she had seen with her own eyes – the carriage, the horses, the chest they had buried in the forest. She would recount everything, except the death of the footman. Her grandmother would know what to do, would know all about the elegant young man who had stepped down onto the footman's grey coat.

A chill wind swept across the land – the high land, above the town, where few people came. It was said that the forest was haunted, a place where witches roamed at night. When Elowen ventured to the marketplace to sell the meat she caught in her traps, she always confirmed to others the worst of the rumours. Her grandmother said it kept folk well away.

'Tell 'em I dance with the devil at night,' she cackled. 'That'll put the fear of 'ell up 'em all!'

By the time Elowen reached her neighbour Ann Netherton's dwelling, Maben was already inside, carefully laying the rabbits and pigeon on the table. The boy was excited – jigging from left leg to right. *What would he be saying if he had sensible words to speak?* Elowen wondered. *Would his voice be softly measured, or as insensible as his movements?*

Ann stood admiring the haul.

'Maben and I thank you, dear Elowen, for these offerings. And I will thank God in my prayers and ask Him to protect you and your grandmother as He protects me.'

Elowen smiled. Ann was considered a good friend, even if her grandmother was wary of Ann's God-fearing nature. As she re-claimed her sack, placing one of the rabbits inside, she wondered why Ann was so devout in her prayer-making and if it was true that non-believers were branded by the devil when they died.

'Thank you, Mistress Netherton,' she said. 'Maben will soon be laying traps of his own.'

'And it will be down to you, Elowen, when he does. He could have no better friend and teacher – that's the truth of it.'

Ann cut Elowen a half loaf of bread just as Bethsany, Ann's older sister, entered, holding an apron of eggs. They looked anything but sisters – Ann tall and slender with fair hair neatly tied in a bun; Bethsany older, heavier and with thick powerful arms, her lank, brown hair riven with iron grey. Elowen had often speculated if Maben was Bethsany's son, but Elowen's grandmother had disputed this, confirming that Maben had been taken in as a babe nearly ten years since – an abandoned waif whose parents had come to grief.

Bethsany transferred the eggs to the table, then set four aside for Elowen, tying them loose in a spare cloth. Elowen bowed her head at this unexpected gift whereupon Bethsany slumped onto a stool with a groan and began shredding herbs she had picked along the water's edge.

'May the Lord protect you and your grandmother,' said Ann. Elowen thanked her and said goodbye, ruffling Maben's head as she left.

It was a short half mile or so to her grandmother's dwelling, a straight steady walk following the stream. Elowen's grandfather had built it, the simple wooden structure made sturdy over the years with thatch and daub. It had once housed Elowen's mother and uncle when they were young, until her mother followed a man and returned to London where she fell into drink and worse. The dwelling, like all buildings in these parts, lay away from its neighbours, a simple place where her grandmother quietly wiled away her days.

As she walked, Elowen admired the stream, its soothing sound lulling her into further thoughts about how Ann's godliness was all-pervading. Ann believed that life was but a period of time spent waiting for Christ's return. It was said that she met with others in a secret church, and that she prayed throughout the night. Perhaps even now – now that Elowen had departed – the three of them were kneeling together, asking forgiveness, asking for respite from war, and from those false religions that demeaned the one true God with their teachings.

The sun burst through the clouds, sparkling the water. Tempted by its purity, Elowen stopped for a moment. She cautiously descended the sloping bank to the water's edge. She knelt and dipped her cupped hands, bringing the pure, clear water to her lips as if drinking from a chalice. It was cold and sweet. *This is my God,* she thought. *The natural world and everything in it.* She offered the stream a blessing, then offered another blessing for the bounty in her sack. She dipped her hands again, threw water onto her face, felt joy with all of life as she prepared to go on her way.

The sound of horses at a distance startled her. She crouched for a while, then slowly clawed up the bank, edging herself towards the crest to see the nature of those who were riding. There were four of them, all wearing the colours of the king. Two of the soldiers she recognised from Old Elijah's dwelling. All were part of the garrison at Pendennis Castle – the great castle that stood high on the isthmus, its turret proudly flying the standard of King Charles for all who sailed towards the harbour to see.

Elowen watched as the cavalry men galloped a wide arc into the forest. Old Elijah had told her that in the town there was talk of soldiers deserting – unwilling to fight a battle they knew they would lose – and for the past few months the garrison's pressgang had scoured the countryside, eager to find new recruits. The soldiers could be rough in their persuading. It was known for boys to be taken from their beds and marched at knife point to the town's recruiting office. Those who refused were beaten. But why had the soldiers returned? Had they heard something new? Had they found the body of the footman lying beneath the leaves?

She lowered her head, giving up her line of sight, and nestled amongst the thin trees until they passed by. When she was certain they had done so, Elowen eased her way onto the trackway, hurrying home in case the cavalry men unexpectedly emerged again.

As she approached her grandmother's dwelling, she saw that the pegged-out clothes hadn't been taken in. After the short burst of sun, it had clouded over again this past half hour and was beginning to spit rain. Usually, her grandmother, who thought it bad luck for newly washed clothes to be set on by rain, would have taken them inside.

Close now, Elowen whistled. She expected Gallant, the dog, to appear, and race towards her at a fearsome pace. But there was no sign of the hound. She reached the door and listened. Something was amiss.

She entered warily. Elowen's grandmother was sitting upright in her chair, her head slumped to one side, her hands clasped together in her lap. Gallant was lying at her feet, whining.

'Grandmother? What ails you? Are you sleeping?'

Elowen went to her, gently nudged her shoulder and stroked her hands, which she discovered were stiff and cold.

The old woman had said that one day Elowen would find her like this – that the old gods would take her without so much as a proper farewell. Elowen offered a final kiss and closed her grandmother's eyes. Then she stood for a while considering the nature of death, how gently and tenderly it sometimes went about its business.

Elowen thought back to those moments before she set off with Maben into the forest. Her grandmother had said she was tired and complained of dizziness but otherwise had seemed content. Now, in the space of a few hours, Death had claimed her. Perhaps Death had taken pity. Her grandmother's life had been marked with sorrow. Her husband had been killed, her eldest son had disappeared. Elowen's mother, her only daughter, had passed on, ravaged by drink and grief of mind. The old woman had cared for Elowen as best she could, teaching her about the secret world that lies beyond the things we see. She stroked her grandmother's forehead and felt tears well in her eyes. Then she knelt and told Gallant to wait patiently until his mistress's return, before running as fast as she was able back to Ann Netherton's dwelling.

3.

(i)

Along the wharf of the ever-expanding Rotterdam harbour, Dan Arent, a broad, bearded man of fifty, was anxiously checking a number of barrels against a written note in his hand. Along with members of his crew he was overseeing the day labourers loading his ship, the *Adventurer*, with its cargo and supplies. It had been a slow process, testing Arent's patience. The River Meuse had been particularly busy throughout the morning with many vessels lying in wait. There had been congestion – crowds of men, lines of pack carts, and angry ship owners marching up and down, all waiting to set sail to different corners of the world. It was midday before the barrels of beef and salted hogs had been safely stored in the *Adventurer's* hold. The cider had eventually arrived in the afternoon and was only now being unloaded, although Arent had already noted the consignment was five barrels short. The cart drivers, of course, knew nothing about missing barrels. Normally Arent would crack heads to discover the truth. But he had more pressing things to worry about. The most important part of his cargo, fifty drums of gunpowder, was nowhere to be seen.

'How much longer before we sail, Captain?'

Arent looked to the ship's deck. Cadwaller Jones, his friend and deputy, was standing against the portside gunwale looking down over the wharf, short, balding, and stripped to the waist, his torso and brow glistening with sweat. Jones and Arent had been friends since their army days, when they fought together in the long war to end the Spanish yoke. He was nearly as old as Arent but in sprightlier shape. The hold was a hot place to work for a man in his late forties, especially if you were rolling barrels. Cadwaller, always eager, and as tough as oiled leather, still managed to do it with ease.

'We won't be sailing at all if the damned powder doesn't arrive!' shouted Arent. 'And there's our money to consider. If the English renege on the deal, then we'll take what we've loaded as payment for our time.'

Jones shimmied down a thick mooring rope, landing a few paces away from Arent.

'I don't trust the bastards!' he said in a forceful tone, wiping his head with a rag. 'It wouldn't be the first time they've changed their plans.'

'Their king is on a losing streak,' said Arent. 'Which is good for us – we can drive a high price from his loyal exiles. But his support won't last. What fool will gamble on a weak king hiding in a corner of Oxford?'

Cadwaller laughed. 'If the powder hasn't arrived in an hour, we'll sink a few barrels of cider and have a hearty night in the town. What do you say?'

Arent knew the options were narrow if the powder was late. They needed to set sail for the channel in day light, then drift easy until dark. Another few wasted hours and it would be too late. A night in town was the last thing Arent wanted. His crew would set themselves to drinking and whoring; he might never see half of them again.

He turned and walked the short distance from the harbour into town, glad to escape from the bustle of loading the ship. In years gone by, he had spent every waking hour attending to his ship's minutest detail. Not so now. The *Adventurer*, a three-masted fluyt, was no longer the all-consuming passion of his life. Only his friend Cadwaller Jones had saved him from a life of dissolution, had convinced him to continue doing what he did best. That was two years ago, when Arent was spending more time in the tavern than on the wharf – a time when he was thrown out of his house and bedded down in the captain's quarters with brandy, rum and ale. Cadwaller had taken him in, eased his friend off ship and into a clean bed; and it was Cadwaller's young wife who, in the months that followed, fed him and tended to his distemper. Arent was thankful to them both for steering him away from the gutter, and worse. But now, as he walked through Rotterdam's narrow streets, he decided that a new life was calling – a life he had once planned together with the woman he'd loved. After the England trip, unbeknown to his deputy, he was going to sell the *Adventurer* and, with the profit, settle permanently on foreign shores.

Arent stopped and purchased a small bunch of flowers from an old woman in the street, then he made his way along a rising pathway that led to the city cemetery. Once through the gate, he settled before a grave near the far fence, a grave sheltered by a drooping elm. Its headstone – weathered by the years – carried three names. Arent wiped each name with his neck scarf, cleaning the stone as best as he was able of any impediment that might cause the lettering to fade.

The grave was the resting place of his wife and two children. Three years had passed since he lost them, three long years during which he had fought, drunk and snarled against the world and everything in it. The fruits of his hard work, his own trading fleet, had disappeared. Contracts had been lost. Money had been frittered away. Two of his three ships had been sold to pay his debts. No longer was he the temperate church-going master of trade he had been when his family was alive, a man of good standing whose word was his bond. Now his reputation was as a hard-drinking miscreant – Dan Arent, the once godly man, who had fallen from faith. And if he were to stand in court to answer for his dissolute life, he would tell those prepared to listen that grief was the root cause of it all; grief and a burning anger at his loss.

He laid the flowers at the base of the grave's simple stone. It was his first visit in several months, a secret that gnawed at his guts. He whispered an apology to his wife, then confessed to her that long hours of consideration had convinced him to recast his life anew. No longer, he said, could he remain in the country of his birth. Guilt was the driver, as well as the memories of their time together. Those memories haunted him, appeared on every corner; the voices of his wife and children seemed to whistle in familiar places, their spirits swirling in the streets. It was this haunting that had done for him, was the reason why moneylenders had reclaimed his house; it was why his ships had been sold and his livelihood gone under. He asked her to understand, asked his children to forgive him. Then he wiped his eyes with his neck scarf, feeling foolish as he did so.

He walked slowly back towards the harbour. There was a time when prayer would have provided him with comfort, perhaps even answers. Not anymore. His faith in God had left him the moment his family was lowered into the ground. That the creator was callously able to take from him the people he loved most was beyond all comprehension. He knew that his wife would have had an answer to it all. 'It is God's way of testing you,' she would have said. His fists clenched in sorrow and anger as, for a fleeting moment, her voice came to him once again. Perhaps, long ago, he might have believed such a thing. Now, her imaginary words struck him as mere platitudes, knitted together to comfort a soul in torment. God had struck a harsh blow and he refused to be cowed. After the voyage to England, Dan Arent would shape his own destiny. And at the earliest opportunity he would make Cadwaller a generous offer that would be a token of gratitude as well as the means of his escape.

(ii)

'Well, well – look over there,' said Cadwaller Jones, nodding towards the harbour toll house. 'A friend of the English king. And he looks to be in a hurry.'

Arent turned and saw a man in a red doublet edging his way uncertainly through the crowd. He was accompanied by two other men – rough types – offering protection. Arent knew the man as Sir Paul Pindar, an agent for the English king's young son, the Prince of Wales. This was whom he had been waiting for.

'Well spotted, Cadwaller,' Arent said. 'Our powder barrels seem to be on their way at last. We may well make sail this evening after all.'

Arent walked through the crowd towards Pindar. The stench of the wharf did not agree with the agent's delicate sensibilities. Tall and somewhat gaunt, he was holding a scented handkerchief to his nose, breathing sweet aromas in fits and starts as if his life depended on it.

Arent caught Pindar's eye and introduced himself. A moment of hesitation followed; Sir Paul stood with a look of surprise, as if expecting Arent to either bow or kiss his hand.

'This really is too, too much,' Pindar said taking another deep scented breath from his improvised nosebag.

'Trade in Rotterdam blossoms,' said Arent. 'And it takes many forms. This, sir, is my ship, the *Adventurer*.' He extended his hand as if offering Pindar the opportunity to gaze upon a great work of art.

'Yes, yes!' snapped Pindar. 'You will be well rewarded for your work on successful completion of the task in hand.'

Arent, irritated at the man's haughty tone, said, 'We've been waiting all morning for powder. I hope you're not going to waste my time, sir, with excuses.'

Pindar began to sway like a mast in heavy wind. 'I cannot speak. I can barely breathe,' said Sir Paul. 'My senses are awash with foul odours.'

'That'll be the fish guts and pig offal and such like,' said Cadwaller Jones with a mischievous grin. 'There's good money to be made shipping the queasy stuff east.'

MARK KILBURN

Sir Paul grimaced. The two roughs stared at Arent and Jones, as if concerned that their charge had been poisoned on the sly.

'Perhaps it is best if we discuss our business on board,' said Arent. Sir Paul gave a sickly nod, and the five men crossed the gang plank onto the ship.

Only Sir Paul and Dan Arent settled themselves in the captain's quarters. The roughs remained on deck; Cadwaller returned to the hold. Sir Paul laid down his kerchief and began to stroke his sharp beard and thin moustache.

'The powder has been subject to delay but is now *en route*. I expect it to arrive within the hour.'

Arent nodded. 'In that case we will be at our destination by morning.'

Sir Paul took out a map from his shoulder bag and unfurled it on the small table, fussing as he looked for something to weigh down the corners.

'The situation in our kingdom has, alas, deteriorated. The king's enemy, Fairfax, sweeps all before him. My current information is that Falmouth remains in Royalist hands – the approaches to the castle are unhampered by Parliamentary ships. There are guns in place to ensure the garrison retains the upper hand. Controlling the approaches to Falmouth harbour is key if the king is to retain a foothold in the south-west.'

'I have heard there have been many setbacks of late,' Arent said.

Sir Paul nodded in agreement. 'The Cornish stand with the king. Our saving grace is that Parliament cannot impose

30

sentiment upon such a loyal body. It is only a matter of time before the pendulum swings once again in His Royal Highness's favour.'

Arent studied the map. The great castle of Pendennis, the depository for the *Adventurer's* cargo, sat some two hundred feet above sea level on a rocky, tree-covered outcrop. Remaining at anchor while supplies were ferried to shore was a dangerous prospect.

'Surprise will be key,' Sir Paul said. 'The governor has plans in hand to seal the mouth of the harbour approach.'

Falmouth, said Pindar, was blessed with a busy, deep-water harbour where ships engaged in trade frequently put in. 'The castle governor is a patriot, a man of honour who will remain steadfast in his service to the king.'

Arent nodded. 'We will not fail you,' said Arent. 'All that is required is our payment.'

'Perhaps first,' said Sir Paul, 'I may be offered a nip of courage, in order to settle my constitution?'

Arent went to a cabinet and took out a cut-glass decanter and two glasses. As he did so, Sir Paul upturned his bag. Several light-brown leather pouches, each filled with gold coin, tumbled onto the table.

'Half of what we have agreed,' he said, forming the pouches into a neat line. 'The rest to be paid upon completion of your mission.'

Arent checked each bag. He knew the king's supporters in exile were having difficulty raising money for their cause. The English queen, Henrietta, had been reduced to exchanging silver plate for weapons. But the much-heralded European army she had put her faith in was proving harder to raise. Few of Henrietta's backers seemed convinced that her husband Charles would return to the throne. The tide of England's civil war had turned against the monarch. Pindar and his band of exiled Royalists were contaminated with an air of desperation.

Arent completed his counting. The amount tallied. He and his crew would make a tidy sum from delivering supplies to Pendennis castle.

'All is in order,' he said and suggested they raise their glasses to a successful voyage.

As Pindar and Arent were about to take a sip of their dark medicinal rum, a breathless Cadwaller Jones appeared at the door with news.

'The gunpowder has arrived, Captain,' he said. Arent thanked his friend for his timely information.

'Your good health, Sir Paul,' he said.

Pindar inhaled a short intake of breath, pinched his nose and drank.

4.

(i)

After her grandmother had been laid to rest, close to the bank of the stream, Elowen stood in what had been her home for the past fifteen years, considering what she might keep for herself. There was little of value – pots, drinking cups, two wooden bowls – nothing substantial that she wished to inherit. She knew she could not stay here. She was the daughter of a drunkard, a woman who had died of grief, and she wished to prove that she was cut from a different cloth. Only her grandmother had offered an insight into her family's redeeming characteristics. The old woman had been honest and hard-working, someone who used their wits and cunning to make their way through life. *Such am I,* thought Elowen. *Such am I.*

She gathered a few possessions, wrapped them in a rough blanket and tied a double knot. That morning, Old Elijah had told her the town was preparing for the worst. Fairfax's Parliamentary army – one of the most fearless armies ever assembled in England – had captured Launceston. Even now Roundhead soldiers were marching along Cornwall's notoriously barren trackways, threatening villages and towns with their powder guns, pikes, and worse. In the coming hours, he said, Truro would be over run. Then it was only a fair morning's march to Falmouth.

'Flee while youse can,' the old man had told her. 'Unless 'e yearn to swing from a forest bower wearing the devil's necktie.'

Old Elijah spoke the truth. What hope was there for a sixteen-year-old girl who lived on the edge of the forest? The Cornish Trained Bands were no match for Fairfax's army. Soon the little town would be awash with Parliament's soldiers and Elowen would be flogged into their ranks. Only one place offered sanctuary: the towering grey castle at the far end of town, known as Pendennis.

And there was something else, a thought she had been turning over and over since her grandmother's death. Was the old woman's passing an act of retribution? Had the forest gods decided to punish Elowen for the killing of the royal footman? A cold realisation took hold. The gods were angry. The forest, the place she held most dear, would surely be out of bounds until she redeemed herself.

With her blanket slung over her shoulder, Elowen brought Gallant to heel. The hound was curious. So many things had changed. He began to pant, eager for affection – affection that his mistress was now unable to give. Perhaps it would be better if the hound followed Elowen's grandmother to the other side of the spirit world where she would be waiting for him. If Ann Netherton refused Gallant a home, that's what Elowen decided must happen.

She left the dwelling and began to walk, following the familiar line of the stream. How she would miss the sweet, cooling taste of the water! How she would miss the sensual atmosphere among the trees in which she had spent so many hours! Anger coursed through her as visions of Roundhead soldiers polluting the grasslands invaded her thoughts — soldiers felling the great oaks to fashion pike rods and baggage wagons, digging the lush saddle of land where she lived to pitch their canons and tents. She wondered what these soldiers looked like, these youths and men who had upended the country — men with horns like her good-for-nothing father, so she reckoned, filled with treachery and dissolution.

Elowen stopped before Ann Netherton's dwelling. Bethsany was scattering seed before an excited ruffle of chickens; Maben was hauling a bucket of water from the stream. The boy gave Elowen a cautious welcome, far removed from his usual eager greeting. Did he already understand that she was about to desert him?

Bethsany called out. Ann emerged with a look of weariness, a weariness that might easily have been mistaken for contempt. Gallant began to whine; Elowen felt herself weaken. She stroked the old dog's ears; Ann, she knew, had been at prayer and Elowen drew breath, resolved that one day she would fix her neighbour's mind on the true nature of the world, not on the untrue nature of how the world should be. But what Ann said to her was a surprise.

'You have come to say farewell,' said Ann, wiping her hands on a kitchen rag. 'A new home awaits you — a fortress of grey stone, I would reason.'

Elowen nodded. 'I would ask you to oversee my grandmother's dwelling, mistress Ann, until I am able to return. And I would also ask that you take care of Gallant, most loyal of animals.'

Maben plunged his hands into the bucket of sweet stream water. Elowen saw that the boy had fished out a wooden bowl. He approached Elowen and offered it to her.

'You will be missed,' said Ann.

Elowen took the bowl and drank. 'I have made my decision, Mistress Ann. The gods of the forest have spoken.'

She handed the bowl to Maben. She knew that Ann would be affronted by such talk. To her, there were no gods of the forest – only the one true God who gathered all righteous souls into His eternal arms.

Elowen continued. 'Whatever provisions and implements in our dwelling you can make use of are yours to choose. I look forward to the day when this foul time has ended, and I am able to return.'

Ann walked up to her and stroked her cheek.

'Wait,' she said. She went inside and returned with a knife, the blade sharp and well-fashioned. She turned Elowen around and pulled out her hair from beneath the collar of her coat.

'What name will you go under?' she asked.

'Elijah.'

'Then let me go to work, young Elijah, so that you might look a great deal more like a man.'

She let loose Elowen's hair, began to draw the blade lightly, shearing the girl's thick locks at a level that ran concurrent to the nape of her neck.

When her hair had been shorn so that it rested on her jacket collar, Elowen thanked Ann and began to walk along the track leading to the town.

'God be with you,' said Ann and took hold of Gallant by the scruff of his neck preventing the hound's natural instinct to follow. Bethsany, aware of Maben's impending grief, placed a strong, comforting hand on the boy's shoulder. And when Elowen was no longer in their sight they tied Gallant to a post with a dish of scraps close by. Then Ann, Bethsany and Maben came together in a close circle to offer up a prayer for Elowen's safe passage and eventual return.

(ii)

Standing high on the grasslands, before the trackway began its descent, Elowen caught a broad sight of the harbour. Ships lay at anchor; smaller boats zig zagged from one side of the land to the other. It seemed a day like any other, except that everyone in the town was waiting for Fairfax's army to arrive. As she made her way down the hill and through a narrow cut in the trees, she came out onto a road – a further steep decline to the town, ending at the market square. There, she saw men, women and children huddled in groups, anxious about what was to become of them. She could have avoided the square but decided to linger awhile. She walked among the traders, listened to their foreboding, side-stepping a boy who was pulling a squealing piglet by a rope as she did so. A fisher woman, her skirts encrusted with dried blood and scales, was shaking her head in a rapid motion as if overcome by a strange visceral madness. Elowen took hold of her calloused hand and the woman calmed herself; then, when Elowen let go, she began her shaking again. All around the marketplace people were shouting, issuing orders, praying for mercy. Elowen moved among them and yearned for the peace of the forest.

'What's to do, father?' she asked an elderly man, a wide brimmed hat fixed to his head, strands of long grey hair veiling his eyes. He smiled, revealing several blackened teeth.

'The devil will soon be upon us,' he said. 'We must take shelter where's we can.'

'And what if I have no shelter to go to?' said Elowen. 'Where then should I hide?'

The old man shook his head and pointed towards the sea.

'Away from 'ere, boy, unless youse wants to end yer days with the staggers.'

Elowen now saw that a steady stream of ragged people were making their way along the high-street. Some were pulling small carts piled high with bedding; others carried their life's possessions in their arms. Elowen, struggling now with the packed blanket on her shoulder, fell into line. This, she thought, is my new life, and she suddenly felt alone in the world.

When she reached the bend near the town's church, she saw in the distance an anxious knot of townsfolk waiting before an imposing grey building. The building was known as Arwenack Manor. A grand house, it had been requisitioned as a Royalist headquarters and border post. Several guards stood shoulder to shoulder, preventing access to the rising castle road beyond as the crowd waited to be admitted into the building. It was here the garrison's commanding officers decided who would be allowed to seek refuge in the castle and who would be turned away.

An hour passed before Elowen was given permission to present herself to three army officials in a ground floor anteroom. She explained that she wished to enlist as a soldier whereupon an officer looked her up and down with a rueful eye.

'Can you fire a musket, boy?' he asked. 'Can you row or sail a boat?' asked another.

Elowen said that she was yet to learn how to fire a musket and had only sailed once in a boat, an experience she tried to forget as the choppy sea waters had sent her into a giddy spin. Aware in the silence that followed that she needed to paint herself in a more favourable light, she hurriedly sought to explain her attributes.

'Tracking and catching animals is my pleasure, sir,' she said, 'as well as being fearsome with a slingshot.'

One of the officers laughed at this. What use would tracking animals be in the confines of the castle? Didn't the boy know that Pendennis had provisions of its own? The boy's case was doomed to fail, they laughed – unless Elowen wished a job as a rat catcher?

'Ay, there's plenty of rats lurking beneath the skirts of women at Pendennis,' said a second officer.

This brought on more laughter. A third official, whose rank seemed to be placed above the others, shook his head, indicating that Elowen should be sent back to the marketplace.

'But I am eager to learn, sir,' Elowen said. 'And I wish above all to serve the king with three feathers.'

The commanding officer looked at Elowen in a puzzled manner.

'How do you know that the Prince of Wales is at the castle, boy?'

Elowen hesitated. 'My grandmother spoke of it,' she said. 'Before she passed on from this life, sir. She had a dream that he would visit. She knew things, sir, things that only a wise woman would know.'

The commanding officer continued looking at Elowen in a strange way. Then, with his quill lingering over a torn piece of parchment, he said to a subordinate: 'Take him through!' and Elowen found herself ushered to the rear of the great manor.

A group of soldiers sat idle in the garden, an array of matchlocks and flintlocks before them. Elowen was asked to choose one. She took up a long-barrelled musket – similar to the one the king's footman aimed at her on that fateful day. The soldiers gave a whistle in recognition of the haughtiness of her manner. A trooper, tall with long flaxen hair, smiled and made a brief aside to his comrades which Elowen didn't understand.

'First, fill your pan with powder,' said the soldier. 'Then pour a small dose into the barrel. Next comes your wadding and ball. See? Set 'em good and proper with your scouring stick.'

Elowen could hear muffled giggles from the other men as she pushed the stick hard into the barrel. Was she being made a fool of? The soldier set the match cord to what he called the serpent on the side of the barrel.

'Now, lad, take good aim, then pull the trigger,' he said, 'and blow old Fairfax to kingdom come.'

A scarecrow hung from a wall thirty or so paces away. The soldiers edged themselves into a corner, out of harm's way. Elowen lifted the musket to her shoulder, aimed and set the trigger. A smoky, fizzing moment elapsed before a forceful explosion knocked her backwards onto the floor.

More laughter. Then the officer stepped forward to examine the hanging ball of rags shaped into a man. Elowen had missed the scarecrow's head by a country mile.

''E's no good!' one of the soldier's shouted. 'A doxy'd do a better job of it!' The flaxen-haired trooper shook his head and told Elowen to make herself scarce as she was best suited to a life picking winkles, not defending the king.

She begged them not to be so hasty. She pulled her slingshot from her waist and found a stone to set into its pouch.

'What's this?' asked one of the soldiers. 'A child's toy, is it not?'

The flaxen-haired trooper pulled Elowen towards him.

'What are you going to do with that, eh? Close up you look a tad less than a boy, would that be right?'

He grabbed hold of her coat collar, then pushed his hand down behind her jerkin to her chest where he fumbled for a while and rubbed his filthy fingers against her flesh.

'It ain't tits you need to check for!' shouted a soldier. 'Put your hand down 'is britches and see what's to find.'

The trooper removed his hand, looked long and hard at Elowen's face.

'Show us what you can do, why don't you boy,' he said and stood with the others ready to pass judgement on

MARK KILBURN

Elowen's keen eye.

She set herself firm, her left leg in front of her right, and swung the pouch of her slingshot – several times more than necessary for entertainment's sake – and let loose the rock. It travelled straight and true over the lawn before severing the head of the scarecrow at its scrawny neck.

The soldiers cheered. The flaxen-haired trooper slapped Elowen on the back.

''E's a dark horse, ain't 'e?' the trooper said. 'A slight un with a keen and honest eye. They'll have youse manning the castle defences, boy, ready to put Fairfax's head on a platter!'

Elowen stood and watched as the troopers examined her slingshot, trying hard to replicate the wonder they had witnessed. Then a shout went up from the ante-room, which immediately quietened the men. Elowen was dismissed from the garden and ordered to join a group headed for the castle.

(iii)

Though she had lived high above the little town nearly all her life, the great castle remained a mystery to Elowen. She had seen it once when, aged twelve, Old Elijah had sat her in a coracle, and they'd sailed out of the harbour so that Elowen might acquire her 'sea legs.' It didn't work. Instead, young Elowen threw up her guts over the side, the first and only time she had ever taken to water.

That day, the castle had loomed over the ocean like a fearsome sentinel – an angry, grey presence, ready and willing to spit fire at invaders, be they French, Spanish or from the darkest ends of the known world. Now the castle was to be a place of refuge for those lucky enough to be granted entry – the last outpost of Royalist resistance in the south-west.

It was a steep climb from Arwenack Manor. The group followed a trackway overlooking the mouth of the harbour. Elowen could see the smaller castle of St Mawes – Pendennis's little brother – protecting the headland opposite, as well as the cold, dark channel beyond. She stopped for a while and admired the expansive view. The accompanying troop of soldiers didn't seem to notice her slacking, seemed content to saunter in front of her and the seven other souls who accompanied her. Four of these were women, granted sanctuary due to family ties with some of the men garrisoned there. On occasion, Elowen caught their whispers and their eyes flickering in her direction.

At the crest of the hill, men were busy firming up the castle's outer defences – ditches, parapets and trenches reinforced with timber. A scrawny gang of youths carried pails of concrete, tipping the mulch onto the ground beside a team of block layers who were shaping white stone. These harsh-looking men, stripped to the waist, hauled boulders from a pile before edging them into position. As Elowen's group passed by, the block layers rested a moment in order to leer at the new recruits who would soon be living amongst them.

The castle's arched gatehouse came into sight. *Where will the fighting take place?* Elowen wondered. Would Fairfax and his army surround the castle walls, use battering rams and erect ladders to gain entry? She knew little of warfare, little of the rules and codes of military life. Some amongst her group laughed off the prospect of conflict, saying an agreement between Parliament and the king would soon be forthcoming. Others said that it was a barren hope to believe in peace, a hope that had been expressed many times since the dirty war began. One woman whispered that bible prophesy was coming to fruition – that Satan and his minions were riding towards them in preparation for the end of time and the holy battle that would right the world.

The castle's portcullis slowly lifted, the ancient hinges groaning in their sockets. Elowen and the others walked across a wooden drawbridge, glancing at the murky water that filled the moat. Once through the main archway, she was met by a scene of great endeavour. The parade ground was teeming with horses, women and children. There were impatient shouts as a line of soldiers tried to secure a place in the barracks room which took up part of a separate block of buildings. Elowen looked up at the first-floor windows: the state rooms, inhabited by the governor and his commanders, and strictly out of bounds. She then gasped at the castle's central tower, pierced with embrasures for artillery and crowned with a turret. *I will be safe in this place*, she thought. *No army will be able to penetrate these thick walls; no Parliamentary general will be able to force the castle's surrender.*

A soldier ordered Elowen and the others in her group to stand in line before a room close to the entrance arch. From what she was able to see, the barracks could accommodate only a small proportion of the garrison. Other ground-floor rooms seemed to have been designated for storage. Elowen looked around the parade ground: where, she wondered, would the rest of the castle's desperate population lay their heads?

It didn't take long before she became aware of the

solution. Soldiers and others were constructing lean-tos and flimsy shelters out of tarpaulin and wood salvaged from the castle stores. She was surprised by the number of women and children. They, too, were helping – dragging items for the shelters' construction or else lighting small fires on which to boil water or cook food.

She was ordered to step forward, ushered into the tiny room. A stern-faced recruiting master sat at a desk. The procedure of enlisting was brief: she was asked a few basic questions – name, age, place of birth – before being ordered to offer up an oath saying that she would faithfully serve the king. She was then taken to a storeroom and issued her uniform: a harsh woollen shirt, britches, a long grey coat, and boots. Weaponry, she was told, would be issued the following day. She was dismissed and told to find shelter as best she could.

Weighed down with her new clothes and the few possessions she had brought from home tied in her blanket, she cut an ungainly figure as she wandered across the parade ground, searching out a space to call her own. A tall, somewhat skinny youth wearing a buff coat, green britches and white stockings called out to her. 'You there,' he said. 'Follow me.'

Such was the determination of the soldiers to construct shelters before nightfall that Elowen was repeatedly cursed and cussed and knocked sideways as she walked from one end of the parade ground to the other. Eventually the youth came to a halt before a lean-to built against a low wall overlooking the castle stables.

'You'll share with me,' said the youth. 'Have you more clothing?'

Elowen nodded.

'Good. The nights get cold here. I use the flags as extra covers.'

Inside the shelter was enough space for two people to sleep. Elowen passed the youth her belongings and he threw them to the right-hand side. A flagpole had been placed in the middle of the shelter in a meek attempt to formally divide the space.

'My name is Thomas Kettleby. I am the ensign. You have been entrusted to assist me in my duties.'

For the first time Elowen looked her colleague up and down. He was older by a few years or so and had long straggly, shoulder-length brown hair. He was thin, she decided, through a lack of nourishment, and his eyes and raspy voice betrayed a nervous anxiety. Whether these deficiencies were due to the impending battle with Fairfax's Parliamentary army or because it was Thomas Kettleby's natural disposition, Elowen wasn't sure.

'I am Elijah, Mr Kettleby. I will assist you as best I can,' said Elowen.

Kettleby seemed satisfied with Elowen's reply, a reply which acknowledged his elevated status.

'This is the regimental flag,' he said, pulling a pole out from the shelter. 'When the fateful hour arrives, we must stand firm and guard the flag to our day's end.'

He unfurled it and Elowen admired the flag's rich but worn tapestry. The crest contained a shield and helmet set within a garland of oak leaves. It gave off a coarse, musty smell that Elowen considered must be the scent of battles past.

'But there is more,' said Thomas, wrapping the flag around the pole and returning it neatly to its position on the floor. 'We have amongst us a guest,' he said.

'A guest?'

'In the state rooms,' said Kettleby in a low tone. Up there, in the building where you hitched your kit. Within those rooms resides one who is heir to the English throne.'

Elowen waited. The heir to the English throne was too vague a term to comprehend.

'The king's son – the Prince of Wales,' said Thomas helpfully. 'He'll be travelling abroad directly, to raise monies for the king's cause.' He unfurled the second flag – a deep blue velvet within which sat lions, a harp and the three white plumes Elowen had seen displayed on the black carriage.

She turned and looked again towards the one-storey building at the far side of the parade ground. Thomas followed her gaze.

'It was all barracks at one time; no longer, now the great battle's near. Much of the barracks has been set aside to store food, ale and powder. That's why the garrison rests here, sleeping under the stars.'

'When will Fairfax come?' said Elowen.

'God in his heaven only knows. But Black Tom will be on his way, that you can depend on. And when he arrives, we'll turn him on his heels back to London, so that the king can rightfully be set upon his throne.'

Thomas, excited by his pronouncement, handed Elowen the Prince of Wales's standard and took hold of the regimental flagpole once again.

'That's why we must guard the flags with our lives, Elijah, until the last drop of blood. We will never surrender to the traitors. Never!'

Elowen watched as Kettleby began to spin the flagpole above his head, drawing admiring glances from those settled on the parade ground nearby. A flautist began to play and Kettleby danced for the crowd, swinging and twirling the flag into the air, kneeling on occasion to reclaim the pole as it fell, all the while increasing his momentum, displaying agility, prowess and control. Elowen was transfixed. She had never seen such a performance. Was this what she was expected to do? Entertain this captive crowd? And the crowd grew – clapping and stamping and shouting its approval. Soon, Kettleby was in the centre of a large circle, a circle that was three or four persons deep. Elowen began to appreciate the number and rank of all those who were present in the castle. There were soldiers and their families, the governor and his commanders, children and animals, the mysterious prince hiding behind silk curtains ... What a rare place I have fallen into, she thought! A place of defiance and good humour, of which her grandmother would surely approve! The crowd cheered as Kettleby finished his routine with a final flourish, launching the flag ever higher into the air before catching it while in a kneeling position. The young ensign acknowledged the applause. Elowen looked up to the first-floor windows, saw a figure turn away, and the silk curtains close. Then an officer barked a sharp order, and the crowd began to disperse.

(iv)

It was an uncomfortable first night sleeping with Thomas Kettleby. He was constantly twisting and turning, mouthing strange words, one of which sounded like 'Mama.' Elowen considered poking him in his back, in the same way Bethsany poked Maben when he was experiencing bad dreams, but thought better of it, lest Kettleby became angry and stripped her of her job as junior ensign.

In the early hours, unable to settle, she crawled out of the small shelter. It was a cool, clear night, heavy with the smell of sea wrack and brine. Across the parade ground, Elowen saw other sleepless souls wandering about near their shelters, hoping to be lulled back to their beds by the sound of an ebbing tide. Beacons had been lit on each corner of the battlements – defiant blazing messages that proclaimed Pendennis Castle remained true to the king. Elowen briefly looked up at the state rooms. All were in darkness, though she thought she saw the shadow of a figure move away from one of the windows.

She walked from the parade square towards the stables, a long wooden building which stood near the postern gate. Living beside an ocean was different to living beside a forest. Even in her new boots, the rhythms of the waves made her feel light-footed. It was as if a strange spell was being cast or an important story was being retold. And the sea breeze that swept up and over the castle's walls tasted of salt and fish scales. The air, Elowen thought, seemed to be somehow thicker than in the forest, swirling above the ocean like steam from Bethsany's broth.

She climbed a rack of steps onto the battlement and stood awhile, peering through an embrasure towards the mouth of the harbour. It was there she had sailed with Old Elijah. The waves had been much stronger then, lifting and slamming the coracle as well as Elowen's guts. The sea had scared her. Its anger seemed out of all proportion. She recalled sitting rigid in the tiny boat, gripping the side, whereas Old Elijah, using an oar as a crutch, had stood strong as if the day was like any other.

'You there, boy! Reveal y'self!'

A night guard – a youth not much older than Elowen – approached in the shadows, brandishing a musket that looked too heavy for him to carry.

'I am Elijah, second ensign to Master Thomas Kettleby,' she said.

The youth looked Elowen up and down, took in her oversized, long coat. He pointed at the slingshot tied around her waist.

'And wha's this 'ere?' he said. 'Don't look nuthin' like a belt, it don't.'

A slingshot that I bear with me, for if I might happen upon a rat,' Elowen said.

The youth laughed.

''E'll need more 'an a slingshot to kill the castle's rats,' he said. 'Theyse like dogs – bigger un dogs, some o' 'em. O'er there's best t' see rats. Theyse come up fra' the shoreline, huntin' food.'

He pointed in the direction of the postern gate. Elowen nodded and thanked him for his help.

He took a step towards her now and offered a leery smile that exposed his broken teeth.

'Best get 'e to a place tha's warm than go a-huntin' rats, boy,' he said. ''Is warm by thar there brazier. An' there's a neat little nook for us both to hide away.'

Elowen turned and hurried down the steps then across the grass to the parade ground. She didn't look back, even though the soldier was shouting and laughing after her:

'Best get thee to bed, boy! An' best keep 'ees boots on, lest they rats take a nibble o' yer toes!'

When she crawled into the shelter, Thomas Kettleby was lying on his back, sleeping soundly. Elowen pulled his blanket into place so that it covered him better, turned away from him and fell asleep.

*

At daybreak, at the sound of the bugle's call, the garrison's soldiers formed up. Elowen and Thomas, each holding a flag, took up positions facing the lines of tired, dishevelled men. An officer in full uniform appeared, having made his way from the state rooms. As the soldiers stood to attention, he walked amongst them, giving a cursory inspection, before ordering the garrison dismissed to its day's work.

The rest of the morning was spent practising sword strokes and pike thrusts. Officers struggled to keep a clear space on the parade ground, the swelling number of women and children camped along the perimeter constantly encroaching on the day's drill. As the soldiers jabbed and swung their weapons, their superiors did their best to feed morale. The curtained walls of the castle, they shouted, were being strengthened to deter Roundheads; canons were being put in place to blast Cromwell back to Huntingdon in the north; it was incumbent on all members of the garrison to defend the perimeter should the traitor Fairfax launch an assault. The women and children gave a great cheer at these fine words. Elowen, flushed with pride, sliced the air with her new sword.

When evening came and the parade ground was filled with the smell of blazing fires, cooked meat and strong ale, Thomas Kettleby left Elowen in their tiny shelter and began to wander around the parade ground, reminding the inhabitants of his flag dance the previous day. He brought back morsels of food which, he told Elowen, had been freely given up.

'The ensign is always well looked after,' he said, dividing bread, pottage and strips of beef between them. 'It is considered lucky to offer gifts to the flag bearer so that he might protect the regimental standard to his best of his ability. Here – eat this. The nights are long in this place. There is much merriment to obscure the deep peril in which we find ourselves.'

Thomas was not wrong. After they had eaten, songs and mournful hymns were sung from all corners of the parade ground. And when the night turned cold, and the fires began to draw down, Elowen struggled to stay warm in the shelter. She slept in fits and starts but was fully woken once again in the early hours, this time by the sound of Kettleby's muted sobbing. She turned to him; he was lying with his back towards her, his knees drawn up towards his chin. Elowen, irritated by this new development, nudged him, hoping to put an end to it. When it didn't end, she tried hard to ignore him, burying her head within the folds of her sheepskin coat which she used as a pillow. But Thomas continued to weep ever louder, eventually the vociferous nature of the ensign's tears proving too much. Elowen placed a hand on his shoulder.

'Sleep, friend,' she said. Thomas said he could not.

Now he turned and faced her. In the dark cold of night, he said: 'We are lambs to the slaughter. Do you not understand, Elijah? Fairfax's army will reign terror upon this castle. And who will help us? There is nowhere to run. I am frightened, Elijah. I am frightened to die.'

There was nothing Elowen could do or say. The ensign's sobbing continued. Even the angry shouts from others nearby did not manage to quell Thomas' fears. Elowen covered her head and ears with the corner of the regimental flag that lay between them. It was her second night at the castle and already new, more disturbing thoughts were beginning to play on her mind.

5.

(i)

Ann Netherton left her dwelling and walked along the trackway beside the stream. Maben bounded ahead of her, alongside Gallant the dog. She watched as they ran across the long grass, Gallant jumping as Maben held a small branch above the hound's head. Each day, Ann visited Elowen's grandmother's dwelling to make sure it remained locked and in good repair. As she did so she heard the echo of Elowen's words: 'When the war is over, I will return and lay my traps in the forest with Maben. And, if I do not return, then I leave the dwelling to you, Mistress Netherton, for all the kindness you have shown me over many years.'

The girl's decision to enlist with the garrison at Pendennis Castle had surprised Ann. The forest and the open land high above the town were all Elowen had ever known. Ann had told her that the war between king and parliament, the fighting and daily squalor that existed further up country, was a world away from their scattered community. But Elowen had countered this by saying the war was now close by and it was her duty to serve the king. Ann could sense the influence of the girl's grandmother and prayed that Elowen might have a change of heart. Even in death, it seemed, the old woman's adherence to strange pagan gods lingered on, gods that she had confused with the mystery of Charles, the king.

The weather was cool; the stream bubbled in its own fruitful manner. Ann arrived at the wood and daub cottage and checked that the front door remained secure. Satisfied that no one had entered, she went in.

A harsh, musty scent greeted her – the smell of encroaching damp in the timbers. Gallant, his tail between his legs, pined as he sloped through the door, looking this way and that for Elowen and her grandmother. Maben was downcast, sad that his only true friend had gone; sad, too, that he had no one to hunt with in the forest.

Once the room was aired, and Ann was satisfied the place remained in fair order, she re-fastened the door and walked the short distance to the grave of Elowen's grandmother. She picked a posy of meadowsweet, tying the stems with twine, and lay it before the simple wooden cross that marked the old woman's resting place. Maben, on Ann's command, stood in silence while Gallant cautiously sought out fresh scents along the stream. When Ann had given up a prayer, she allowed Maben to run free, the boy moving awkwardly, twisting like a spinning top that was sure to topple over.

Ann worried for him. His status as a mute and his natural inclination to stray meant that she and Bethsany had to be strict. When the three of them visited a house in the town, joining members of their congregation for prayers, Bethsany was constantly slapping the back of the boy's hands to stop his infernal fidgeting. During bible readings, he had a habit of giggling at certain passages, disturbing the other congregants. Ann hoped that her church would be the boy's salvation; but his inability to fully embrace the Lord made her anxious for his future.

'Maben – we must return. Come now.'

The boy, along with Gallant, had drifted towards the threshold of the forest. He seemed cautious, as if something preyed on his mind.

'Maben!' she called. He turned and skipped ahead, stick in hand, the dog jumping and snapping to retrieve it. 'Go gentle, Maben! Go gentle!' shouted Ann.

It was said the boy's parents were poor tinker folk who drowned in a scully boat, leaving twin babes alone in the world. Ann remembered the day ten years ago when members of her congregation stood at her door, imploring her to come to the town's church where two tightly wrapped new-borns had been found next to a grave. Because Bethsany shed no blood and would always remain without child, the sisters took one in. The other twin, a girl, lived in the town, or so Ann had been told. Whatever the case, Ann had insisted there be no contact between them. Maben was a child who had no need for the influence of a sister.

Gallant began to bark. Across the grasslands, Ann saw two horsemen riding at pace towards them – cavalrymen, wearing the colours of the king. She rushed to the boy, holding tightly to his arm as the soldiers approached. Gallant snarled at the horses, a chestnut mare and a grey. Ann tried to quieten the dog, bending low to take him by the scruff of his neck as the riders brought their mounts to a standstill before her.

'You are from these parts, good wife?'

The soldier spoke with a gamely accent.

'We are godly folk, sir,' Ann said. 'We live but a short way along the stream.'

'Then I must tell you, you are in peril. General Fairfax's army is but hours away. No woman will be safe upon its arrival.'

'My destiny lies in the hands of our Lord, Jesus Christ,' Ann said.

'The Lord won't help you when Fairfax's men come a-callin',' said the second.

Ann did not answer. She was still holding Maben who seemed transfixed by the men and their horses – their stirrups, plumage and colourful tunics – the sheer majesty of the animals bearing down on him. But Ann could not keep hold of Gallant. The dog broke loose, arched himself, began to snarl and bark causing unrest among the horses, bringing the encounter to an early close.

'Heed what we say, good wife. Your God will not spare you from Satan's army.'

They pulled away, riding at a brisk canter. Perhaps they were tasked with finding recruits among the smallholders, thought Ann; or else they were rogues on their way to demand more cider from Old Elijah.

As she walked, she said a quiet prayer, silently admonishing the soldiers for declaring her a "good wife". Ann was no man's wife. She had placed herself firmly in the hands of the Lord, even though she was inclined to believe there were many good men who would court her.

Bethsany came into view bearing a hen from the coop and Ann scolded herself for presuming that she had been blessed above all others.

A pot was boiling on the stove; a square of cheese, bartered at market that very morning, sat beside a slice of cornbread. Fairfax and his army would not encroach upon their lives, Ann was sure. What use to a man like him were two sisters, a mute boy, and a dog?

(ii)

The image of the footman played on Maben's mind. At night he would cry out and flail in his bed, causing Bethsany to get up and calm him with a well-intentioned pinch of his arm. And during his waking hours, as he collected water in the pail or threw grain to the chickens, the footman's face appeared to him in the trees, displaying a fearful look as the force of Elowen's slingshot stone reverberated through the man's body. Did he still wear that fearful look, having lain buried these past days? Or had his grimace transformed itself into a gaze of everlasting serenity?

One day Maben left his chores and walked into the forest. He followed the track towards the road where the Prince of Wales's carriage had come to a halt. Maben looked for the horses that he had set free, wondering if they were grazing beyond the woodland on the opposite side of the road. Slowly he edged towards the place where he and Elowen had piled leaves and branches high on the body of the brutish footman.

The burial mound was still mostly intact. Wind, rain and wild animals had left the top leaves scattered and sodden; branches had been gnawed, pulled to the side. Maben stood over the flimsy burial chamber and began to remove the foliage from above the footman's head. The foul stench of the body came in a rush, causing Maben to retch. As he worked, one arm held across his mouth, the sky clouded over and a squall of rain swept overhead. Gradually, from beneath the tangle and darkness, the footman's face emerged. It had turned a ghastly blue and Maben saw insects swarming across the sunken, blood-drained cheeks. The eyes remained shuttered, the lids still held in place by Elowen's stones, and the purple-coloured mouth remained frozen as tiny motes scurried across the lips.

Maben pulled away more branches until he could see the footman's sodden grey long coat; then he saw the man's white stockings and buckled shoes. Maben liked the look of those shoes. They would fetch a pretty penny in the town market. But he remembered Elowen's words: she had warned him against taking any of the brute's possessions. Why, even the musket had been left behind, a fair prize that would be of interest to many a trader. It lay beside him still, like a lonely, weather-beaten guard.

Maben grew uneasy. And yet death had cast its spell. He wanted something that he could keep, that would absolve his secret.

Again, he heard Elowen's voice. 'Maben,' she had said. 'Plain sight of the footman's possessions will lead to our unmasking as his killers. And if that's the case ... well, think on it! We will be strung up in the market square like dogs.'

He turned away from the buckled shoes and musket. He could tell that the body had lost its firmness; it swilled as if it had turned into pottage. The stench was unbearable, even though the great coat, stained as it was, shielded Maben from the worst. The boy slipped his hand into each pocket; in the first he found wet powder and match cord; and in the second he fished out a small key.

Maben was no fool. He knew what the key was for. He stood with it in the palm of his hand, began to retch once again, the air swirling now with the body's foul odours. He threw the branches, leaves and whatever else was to hand onto the burial mound. Satisfied, he hurried into the forest, among the sweet-smelling pines, where he at last uncovered his mouth and once again breathed freely.

6.

(i)

A sharp northerly wind whistled across Pendennis headland as the small group made its way towards the castle's southerly postern gate. Dusk was beginning to dull all sense of day; a storm had been forecast and the men, women and children who slept on the parade ground were preparing their flimsy shelters for the night rains to come.

The six figures walked quickly; three, unaccustomed to being out in such foul weather, held their cloaks tightly around their necks. The guards patrolling the battlements bowed as the group passed by, cautiously following the movements of the six until the last member had left the confines of the castle and disappeared among the trees. Now the group had to negotiate not only dense woodland but a sloping narrow trackway which would lead them to the rocky shore far below. As the expanse of sea came into view – a brooding sea on the edge of restlessness – one of the men raised his arm and called a halt.

'A draught,' he said, and a velvet bag embossed with three feathers was immediately produced, a bag containing a silver flask filled with French brandy. The cap was unscrewed and, with a bow, Sir Abraham Shipman handed the flask to the impatient figure.

'Your highness …' said Sir Abraham. 'I beseech you – darkness will soon be upon us, rendering our pathway out of sight.'

The young man who took hold of the flask was the tallest amongst them. His black hair fell in ringlets beyond his shoulders and his flamboyant clothes – velvet pantaloons, an embroidered waistcoat of satin, a white shirt brimming with frills – had been made by the king's tailors, the best in the land. He savoured the brandy, enjoying a rich mouthful of the liquor. The others looked on.

'Your highness …'

The flamboyant young man snapped.

'I am aware, Sir Abraham, of the rapidly fading light! I am also aware that I am in need of sustenance in order to make this perilous journey.'

Sir Abraham bowed and decided it would be prudent to say no more. A short, pernickety man with a well-oiled moustache, he stood waiting in silence until such time as he was able to return the silver flask to its bag.

There was a flash of light. Somewhere, out at sea, a torch had been lit. With the help of a piece of leather, or perhaps a cloak, the torch was covered, uncovered, and covered again, relaying a coded message.

'Is that the signal?'

Another man, Major General Molesworth, answered in the affirmative.

'Our contact indicates that a small boat is now safely in its allotted place.'

'Then the Lord has spoken,' said the younger. 'The die for this project is cast. I have been issued word to leave this most sacred isle.'

Finally, Sir Abraham took hold of the flask and replaced it in its bag. The group moved onwards.

Three other figures were discreetly in attendance. All were soldiers, garrisoned at the castle. The shorter of the two was Elowen, her greatcoat and breeches drowning her slender frame, her hands gripping the royal standard. She had volunteered to accompany this most important guest to his tender after Thomas Kettleby had refused to leave his bed. Richard Arundell, the governor's son, and *de facto* Lieutenant-Governor, had given Thomas a stern talking to, telling him to pull himself together else he'd be hung by his neck-scruff and left to the mercy of Fairfax. The youth had pleaded fever – 'a fearsome ague, sire' – to which Richard Arundell had growled that men had fought and won wars suffering worse. Seeing that the chief ensign was resolute in the severity of his disorder, Elowen volunteered to carry the Prince of Wales's standard and accompany the heir to the English throne as he fled, perhaps forever, overseas.

The torchlight message blinked again – short, rapid flashes, more pronounced to the eye in the encompassing darkness. Sir Abraham ordered the lead soldier, and flame bearer, to send a message in response. Taking a breath, the velvet bag was summoned for a second time. They had reached a clearing – the final stretch of pathway to the sea. All was now in place for the prince's departure.

As the prince drank and the soldier struggled in the wind to fashion a flame, Elowen turned and looked upwards in order to fully see the harsh gradient they had descended. The castle walls were obscured by trees and yet the singular knowledge that such a fortress existed high on the peninsula was enough for her to feel a warm glow of belonging. The grey granite that formed the castle's curtained walls compared most favourably against the dark jagged rocks below them which lay beyond the edge of land, lapped over by the sea. Those rocks would slice a man to pieces if he happened to tumble overboard. Many stories had been told of ships that ran aground, their hulls snapped, their rigging brought down, as sea conspired with rock to scuttle them. No army could breach the castle from the southern-most wall, thought Elowen. Cannon and musket fire would send Fairfax's army tumbling into the brine. She took a deep breath and gripped the standard that displayed the crest of the Prince of Wales. Thomas had said the king might well be in retreat, but he was sure an end to the war was near. Whatever their differences, England would always cherish its Parliament and king.

It was at this moment that Elowen saw a figure amongst the trees. It was the figure of a young girl, aged perhaps nine or ten years. Her long, matted hair hung across her face and her clothes were rough and filthy, like those of a wharf vagabond. She seemed to radiate a strange aura: a white mist enveloped her, and her only. Elowen walked forward, such was her curiosity, in order to see more clearly this ghostly figure standing half-way down the steep hill. But the girl disappeared like a wisp among the trees leaving Elowen straining her unbelieving eyes, wondering if the figure had been an apparition or a trick of the light. Then, a second figure appeared – taller, broader, running at speed. The steep gradient was propelling him (for Elowen was in no doubt it was a man) with uncontrollable force in the direction of the group. The figure was also raggedly dressed, with long hair and an unkempt beard. But he did not possess the ghostly aura of the girl. His was the form, Elowen decided, of a madman – a madman intent upon causing great harm.

In the few seconds that elapsed, Elowen saw the flash of a blade. The lead soldier had, by now, lit the torch; flickers of firelight were sent in the direction of a man Elowen now considered to be an assailant. At once she dropped the standard. With both hands free, she drew her slingshot and readied it to fire a small rock at the very moment the dishevelled demon passed by. For the attacker's focus was not on Elowen, nor was it on any of the lesser members of the group. His eyes were fixed firmly upon the Prince of Wales. The future king, she realised, was prey to an assassin.

Elowen whipped the leather band three times above her head and let go her ammunition. The assassin's eyes were demonic, raised to a level of hatred that was unfathomable and beyond comprehension. The rock smacked against the man's cheek bone, tearing his flesh in the same way that Bethsany chopped mutton. A shout went up from Sir Abraham as Elowen, trying to recover the hilt of the flag as the assassin's momentum carried him forward, collided with the savage and was dragged unceremoniously to the ground. And yet, even though he was horribly wounded, the man began to shout in the direction of the prince.

'Death to the murderer!'

The noise soon transformed into hideous death throes, gurgling screams and agonies that seemed to carry on the wind over the wide expanse of ocean.

Elowen's hand kept itself tightly clenched around the flag hilt as the second soldier fell upon the man. She found herself grappling with the assassin's flailing legs. Sir Abraham came forward and stood over the cur, demanding to know the names of those behind such a brazen plot. But the madman was no longer able to formulate his words as blood and bile filled his throat.

'Speak!' Sir Abraham demanded. 'Speak, cur!'

The prince, who was being shielded by Major General Molesworth, now began to edge closer to his would-be killer. He seemed intrigued, looking down at the man as if he were considering a writhing specimen plucked from the animal or insect world. The second soldier drew his sword and asked for the order to dispatch the wretch with a stab to the throat. Sir Abraham ordered him to wait.

'Let me look upon him,' said the prince, 'before this foul individual receives his rightful reward for such a deed. Pity, pity us all – such is the godless state of our once mighty nation.'

'Your highness,' Sir Abraham said. 'We must make good speed now. For who knows what other criminal acts may have been plotted against you.'

The prince ignored him. Suddenly his attention turned to Elowen who remained prostrate on the ground. She had managed to dislodge herself from the traitor's body only for a thin shower of the man's blood to settle upon her hair, face and greatcoat.

'Pray, stand, brave soul!' ordered the prince and Elowen did so, bowing and feeling inadequate under the lucid gaze of majesty.

'What is your name?'

'Elijah, your majesty.'

The prince took in the young soldier's ill-fitting coat, muddied and now dripping blood.

'Well, Elijah. You have proved yourself to be a young man of courage. It is because of you, acting through God's will, that I have life enough to complete my journey. You have my solemn word you will be well rewarded for this courageous act.'

Elowen stared at the prince in a moment of adoration. This was the divine figure who had stepped down from the carriage onto the footman's long-coat; the figure that had majestically been lifted onto the black horse by the carriage drivers; the king-to-be whose protector she had murdered in a similar fashion.

The lead soldier gave a shout – he had managed to send a signal to the waiting ship. Sir Abraham and Major General Molesworth remained close to the wounded assassin despite the man's fearful shrieks.

'I will give you instructions, Sir Abraham,' said the prince, 'with regard to our young ensign. Valour is a sign of grace, is it not?'

Sir Abraham mumbled his answer. 'Your highness, the tender awaits, ready to ferry your esteemed majesty to the *Phoenix*.'

The prince held out his hand, a sacred invitation, to

Elowen, who promptly leaned forward and kissed it.

'Now,' he said, 'let us make good our departure.'

Once she had gathered the royal standard, Elowen followed the prince and his retinue to the rocky shore. The second soldier remained where he stood, his foot clamped hard against the assassin's neck.

As the tendering boat came into view, a series of blood-curdling screams pierced the evening air over which Sir Abraham and Major General Molesworth shouted: 'God save the king!' several times. And when the prince was escorted over the rocks and onto the smaller vessel, Elowen looked up beyond the trees to where she had seen the young girl until the assassin cried his last and was no longer of this world.

(ii)

That night, Elowen told Kettleby about the incident with the fearsome attacker. Still suffering with a high temperature, Kettleby lay shivering in his bed, his face gaunt, his eyes ringed with darkness, while Elowen patted his forehead with a cold flannel.

'Were you scared, Elijah?' he asked.

Elowen said she was not.

'I saw the wretch emerge from amongst thin trees. He proved to be a lumbering target for my sling shot. He was travelling at good speed, I grant you, on account of the steep descent. But he kept to the straight, so the advantage rested with me. A hare is much cleverer: a hare will zig and zag, this way and that, keeping a hunter on his toes.'

Kettleby sighed.

'You are so brave, Elijah. The desire to hunt eluded me when I was a boy. I was more inclined to the kitchen, helping my ma and sister, God rest them, with the food.'

Elowen reached outside the shelter and dipped the flannel in a bowl of fresh water that she had placed by the entrance. A low murmur of night sounds echoed around the parade ground. She looked towards the governor's rooms: a light was flickering. Sir Abraham Shipman and Major General Molesworth, she thought, were now in conference with the governor, telling him the tale.

'Tell me, Elijah, about the prince. Is he as handsome as we are led to believe? Or sickly like his father, the king?'

Elowen wrung out the flannel, relishing the cold water as it washed over her hands.

'I have never set eyes on the king,' she said as she crawled into the shelter. 'Yet I saw in the young prince's eyes great wisdom; wisdom which he will use in service of his subjects. It is as my grandmother used to say: *our loyalty is to majesty and majesty must guide our actions.*'

Kettleby stared at the young ensign.

'Your heroism, dear Elijah, only serves to highlight my own failings. While you were in mortal peril I lay here, in my bed. And now Arundell the governor will promote you to the highest rank, I am sure of it. I am not worthy of my position, Elijah. I have become a mockery.'

Elowen set down the flannel and brushed Kettleby's sweat-ridden hair from his forehead with her palm.

'When I am summoned to the governor's chambers I will tell him that it was because of your good guidance that I felt able to escort the prince safely to his tender.'

Kettleby smiled.

'I will soon be well again, Elijah. And I will show my true mettle for you to see.'

She held his hand until he drifted into sleep. Then she crawled out of the shelter into the night. The conference in the governor's chambers was still ongoing so she decided to walk for a while around the castle grounds. There were many members of the garrison sitting around fires, supping ale or stew, even though it had gone midnight. The southernmost gate had been locked as soon as she, the two soldiers, Sir Abraham Shipman and Major General Molesworth had returned. She could see the night guards walking to and fro along the curtained walls. Elowen thought of the raggedy girl she had seen amongst the trees. Was the assassin her father? Her brother? Where was she? Elowen yearned to know.

She went to the gate and called up to the night-watch. He was slow in showing himself, the result, she thought, of a sleepy head. He peered out from the battlement.

'Who shouts?'

Elowen presented herself and asked to be let through. But the watchman refused.

'You'll need permission from the governor,' he said, his young face stern, unyielding.

'I escorted the prince,' said Elowen. 'And I saw a girl roaming beyond these walls.'

The watchman looked seaward, as if a quick scouring of the dark headland with its thicket of trees would settle the matter.

'No girl that I can see!' he shouted. 'Wait 'til morning. Daytime's better for searching. The headland's alive with beasts an' all manner of unholy things at this hour.'

He disappeared behind one of the square crenelations. Elowen put her ear to the locked gate. The raggedy girl was out there somewhere, and she would find her.

7.

(i)

The *Adventurer's* path through the narrow channel of the Meuse tributary was made slow due to the number of ships entering Rotterdam harbour. Dan Arent had witnessed numerous collisions over the years and was not about to take any chances. From the ship's bridge he bellowed orders to keep the vessel on course and sail within a slow, even speed. Cadwaller stood on the prow shouting and waving at smaller vessels to keep their distance. Leaving port with 58 barrels of gun powder on board, Arent cut a nervous figure, eager for the *Adventurer* to taste the open sea.

Once the ship had finally navigated Rotterdam's approaches and was at full sail, he retired to his quarters. He reached into his leather knapsack and took out Pindar's map which he unfurled across the captain's table – a map of Cornwall, that rugged county situated at the south westerly tip of England, and which, more specifically for Arent, showed Falmouth town nestling on the more temperate side of the coastline.

Arent studied the inlets and approaches of this rocky outpost. The English Parliamentary forces were, according to Pindar's most recent intelligence, still three days away from Falmouth. There would be no need to sail into the small town's harbour, Pindar had told him. The *Adventurer* would be able to drop anchor and allow the cargo to be ferried to shore by skiff. It was easy money and Arent had no doubt that the king's foppish emissary would require further crossings.

'A prolonged war in the south-west could make you a wealthy man, Mr Arent,' Pindar had said. 'Further sailings might require the transportation of mercenaries as well as powder.'

Arent turned and gazed out of the porthole, admiring the great expanse of dark green water. The light was beginning to fade and the sea remained calm; the *Adventurer* was making good time. Their arrival in Cornish waters was scheduled for dawn. Once unloading was complete they would follow the same course home. By tomorrow evening Arent's crew would be celebrating with pork and beer in one of Rotterdam's backstreet taverns.

He opened a small cabinet, set flush in the ship's timbers, poured himself a glass of rum, and drank it down in one. His eyes settled for a moment on his own image, reflected in the small mirror that hung above the washbasin. It was the image of a lonely, middle-aged man – a man who had tasted success, who had lost everything he held dear; who had descended into the gutter and who, against the odds, had risen once again. He slumped in his chair. What was it the Scriptures said? *Whoever hastens to be rich will not go unpunished.* Arent had been punished once and he wasn't interested in being punished again. Pindar's offer of wealth no longer seduced his ears. After all, recouping the fortune he had lost seemed a trivial undertaking. What would he do with it? Spend it on long boisterous nights? More ships? Find himself a substitute wife who would bear his substitute children? Arent had no wish to return to domestic life, in the same way that he had no desire to become a lackey of the English king. He knew how war could turn a man – how hatred and violence distilled a foulness of temper that never left, even when war was done.

He refilled his glass. His life had come to a crossroads. The silent prayer that he had uttered on his last visit to the graveyard was a prayer asking for forgiveness. In hushed tones, he had spoken to his wife, explained to her that he had lost the faith she had instilled in him and, because of it, felt ashamed. Then he whispered to her his plans, how he had decided that, on completion of the *Adventurer's* trip to Cornwall, he would end his association with the sea, using whatever profit came into his hand to seek out a new life, away from war-ravaged Europe, away from the heartache he had endured for so long. He whispered that he had thought long about such an adventure, reminded her that it was a dream once shared by her too – to live on foreign shores in a white stone mansion, colonnaded, with a vast tropical garden. There, she once told him, she would build a church and their children would help her do the work of the Lord. Now, even though he was faithless, Arent had identified a place where he could atone for the past, a place where he might build a church that would stand as an everlasting memorial to the only woman he had loved.

A knock at the door disrupted Dan Arent's thoughts. Cadwaller entered, eager to give his report. The night watch was in place, he said. Visibility was good; conditions favourable; a clear sky, a low moon, a fair wind. Few ships had been sighted.

He stopped and stared at his friend. 'You look pale, Captain. Are you ill?'

Arent smiled, reached for a second glass. 'No. I'm not ill. Pour yourself a drink and sit down. I want to talk.'

Cadwaller did as he was asked. In the three years he'd known Dan Arent, he'd witnessed the man's grief as well as his descent into dissolution and eventual re-engagement with everyday life. Now he suspected another twist in the captain's ever-changing mood.

'What is it? Tell it straight,' he said. 'You'll get a fair hearing from me.'

Arent nodded. Cadwaller, he knew, would speak his mind, would give honest opinions when honest questions were asked. And yet it was with difficulty that Arent began to explain the reasons behind his decision to give up his life as a sea trader. The East Indies offered bright new beginnings, he said; a chance to live in peace without the stain of war and its inevitable misery. And he wanted to honour his wife in the only way he knew.

He drank his rum and said these things with the same broad smile and easy manner that had once seduced merchants and investors to place their money into his ships. But the look on Cadwaller's face suggested that Arent's new beginnings were tainted with treachery and deceit, all at the expense of a friend.

'And what's left for the likes of me when you've gone?' said Cadwaller.

'The *Adventurer*, that's what's left for you,' said Arent.

'You're offering a sale?'

'Why not? You know the ship as well as any man. You know the trade. It's an opportunity.'

'We act as a team,' said Cadwaller. 'Each assigned to his role. You deal with merchants. My job is on deck and below.'

Arent's enthusiasm began to diminish as he took in Cadwaller's growing anger. His friend continued:

'Ownership's not for me. Perhaps you think I'm a rich man, sitting on a pretty fortune that I keep to myself – is that it?'

'No,' said Arent. 'There are ways and means … an arrangement of some kind can be hammered out.'

'What? A loan? With interest? I have a young wife and three children. It is all I can do to keep a roof above our heads.'

'Pindar speaks of many trips – lucrative trips, ferrying troops to the south-west of England.'

'And you believe him? That measly peacock? Today there's trade to be had. Then tomorrow – what will there be? Wars turn in an instant. Next month the English king might be rotting in an English gaol. What will become of Cadwaller Jones, vice-captain of the *Adventurer*, then? Out on the street with his starving wife and children, that's what.'

'So,' said Arent. 'I'm the only one permitted to carry such a burden upon my shoulders? Is that what you say?'

'You are a man who is naturally at ease setting a price with traders, who sits easy in the captain's chair.'

'That was in the past,' Arent snapped. 'I no longer yearn to fill those roles. I'm no longer a young man. Now I wish to exchange cold icy storms for sun and simple living. I have decided. I will turn away from it all.'

Cadwaller stood. 'I have no interest in it. There'll be no arrangement. I'm a sailor with children to feed. An honest day's work and an honest wage is all I ask.'

Arent thumped the table. 'Wait!' he said as Cadwaller made for the door. 'Hear me out.'

'There's nothing to hear,' said Cadwaller. 'You've a short memory, Dan Arent. Perhaps the months spent in my home meant nothing to you.'

The two men locked eyes. Arent, knowing his temper was high, hesitated before he answered. During his darkest period, that time after his wife and children were so cruelly taken, Cadwaller had supported him in his time of grief, clearing a room for him in his narrow, rented three-storey house, situated in one of Rotterdam's less prosperous streets.

'You well know there is no truth in what you say,' said Arent. 'It pains me to hear such words.'

He recalled those desperate days, lying drunk in his room, sweeping away the offer of food from Cadwaller's wife. His own home had been sold, the proceeds frittered away. Two of his ships had been impounded by officers of the guard.

'I will forever be thankful, my friend. But I have made my decision. If you will not purchase the *Adventurer*, there are others who will.'

'Then go and find these "others",' said Cadwaller, 'and turn aside those who look to you for their sustenance.'

He slammed the cabin door behind him. Arent took a deep breath. He stared for a while at Pindar's map in an effort to regain his composure, tracing the *Adventurer's* course with the finger of a shaking hand. Then he poured a third cup of rum, drank it down, and then a fourth. Finally, he swept the map and the glass onto the floor and prepared himself for sleep.

(ii)

Arent's sleep that night was an uncomfortable one, plagued once again by dreams lapping against the shoreline of memory – dreams that turned into bitter ugly swells, each crashing wave an accusation of guilt.

It was a ship that put an end to Arent's wife and children – a frigate that mistook the vessel his family were aboard for Irish rebels or royalist plotters. Arent's wife, a pretty, fair-skinned woman, devout in her faith and devoted to her children, had boarded a ketch bound for France. That fateful day she was sailing to Brest to spend the summer with her family – well-to-do Protestant merchants. Arent had cited work in order to defer joining them on the voyage. It was no secret he found her parents glum and judgemental – easy with their damning attitude towards folk whose faith they questioned.

Now, with rum on his breath and sorrow in his brain, they came to him like spectres. His children stood before him: his daughter pretty like her mother, his son a stern-looking captain-to-be. Behind them, her face a white mask of death, stood his wife.

'Look at them,' she said. 'The children you allowed to sail without you. I pray God you remember them, my husband. I pray God you remember me.'

Arent cried out, snatching at breath, his brow beaded with sweat, the ship's timbers aching and groaning as the *Adventurer* ploughed through the night seas. He gripped the side of his bed, heaved himself towards the wash basin where he cupped his hands and splashed water on his face, desperate to assuage himself of his terrors. He had endured the same dream for the past three years, since the day he stood in the cemetery and watched his family lowered into the ground. Drink had once numbed the worst of it, until drink had begun to terrorise him in a wholly different way.

He gathered himself, took a number of deep breaths, and stared through the porthole at a clear, moonlit sea. Soon he began to feel certainty in his decision to seek a new life. After all, how else could he repay his family after so many years of pain?

8.

(i)

On a bright March morning in 1646, Sir Thomas Fairfax's army rounded the bend of the road where the Prince of Wales's carriage had staggered to an inglorious halt. The army was marching with standards raised, to the sound of pipes and drums. The day was warm, the soldiers were in good humour; victory was in sight. Fairfax rode at the head of the long column on his red roan alongside Colonel Fortescue, his deputy. A surprisingly slender man, Fairfax was without helmet. His striking black hair and dark features had astounded the Cornish men and women who'd peered out of their flimsy dwellings to catch sight of the great general as he passed through Cornwall's towns. 'Black Tom! Black Tom!' they murmured, unsure if he was the devil incarnate or a liberator from a far-off foreign country. Those few who held for Parliament bowed in a show of deference; others simply fell to their knees and prayed to God for deliverance from such evil.

After Fairfax had defeated the Trained Bands in the battle of Launceston, further conflict had been avoided by freeing all prisoners and gifting them a shilling along with an official pass home. The general's mercy had bestowed upon the Roundhead army much needed trust. Truro surrendered without a shot being fired. The way was now clear for Fairfax to secure the south-west for Parliament. Only Pendennis Castle, with its aged and stubborn governor, Sir John Arundell, remained defiant. But 'Black Tom', Parliament's leading general, was in no hurry to lay the fortress to waste. 'If needs be', he told his commanders, 'we'll sit a good while and starve the old wretch out.'

The last of the long line of soldiers passed the spot where the black carriage with three feathers had come to grief, the drumbeat, pipes and footfall of a thousand men pulsing the leaves and branches at the hillock's crest. The carriage had long since disappeared – dragged into the countryside by land wreckers who promptly dismantled the royal vehicle piece by piece, selling it off as gaudy tat. All that remained of that fateful morning was a small grave where the chest had been buried, along with the footman's burial mound, hidden behind the tall grass near the threshold of the forest.

Fairfax was tired, eager to reach Falmouth. The small town with its deep harbour would play an important role in policing the Cornish coast. Even now Vice Admiral Batten's Parliamentary ships were in full sail from Portsmouth, ready to impound any Royalist vessels that might be lurking. The slippery young Prince of Wales had already made good his escape – a figurehead for King Charles' exiled supporters to rally around. Parliament needed to deal a blow against these aristocratic meddlers. Any sign of foreign troops making ready to land on English soil would be ruthlessly dealt with.

A mile from Falmouth a scout appeared, galloping from ahead. He pulled up sharply, his grey mare rearing in excited anticipation of the news its rider was about to relay.

'General, I have received reports that the market square is now filled with local men and women.'

'Armed?'

'No, sire. They await your arrival, ready to pay you homage.'

Fairfax nodded and ordered the soldier to re-join his scouting party. *Pacify the local population with acts of kindness and order will follow* was Fairfax's edict. The Cornish, he knew, knelt willingly for the king. They were a strange, far-away people with uncultured thoughts. Cornwall was a place of witchcraft, too, so he'd been told, in which ravens were hung from trees and the ghosts of shipwrecked sailors wailed on the night sands. But the general also knew that poor men were easily swayed with promises of peace and prosperity. Fairfax was in no doubt: Pendennis Castle would surrender within the week.

(ii)

The information the scout delivered to Fairfax was not entirely correct. Only a small number of the folk gathered in the marketplace were prepared to pay homage to the famous general. Others remained in a state of anxiety, assured through months of rumour that Satan himself was about to enter the town. The tiny brick-built cottages that stood near the wharf were either deserted or boarded up, the inhabitants cowering inside. There was no route for them to the safety of the castle. After the last Royalist soldiers in the town had fled behind the castle's walls, the drawbridge remained firmly closed to those souls who stood begging for shelter. For some, the prospect of murder, rape and the foulest torture at the hands of Fairfax's army was overwhelming. They, too, fell to their knees begging God's mercy, smearing their faces with dirt to validate their faith.

The road leading to town was a steep descent. As the troop marched, their drums and pipes could be clearly heard in the town square, causing much consternation. Bethsany, having arrived at market early to sell freshly slaughtered chickens, beckoned Maben towards her. She was sitting on a wooden crate, and positioned the nervous boy between her legs, tucking him into her long skirt. He covered his ears as the army approached and Bethsany comforted him as best she could. Around the perimeter of the square those too old or too frail to leave their squalid dwellings gawped or else offered a hesitant greeting as the scouting party appeared. *Do with us what you will,* they seemed to say. *We stand helpless before you.*

Fairfax had given strict orders that the populace was to be treated with a reasonable hand. He sat graciously in his saddle, allowing himself the pleasure of a gentle nod to those who knelt as he came into view. His soldiers were ordered to confront only those ne'er-do-wells who carried weaponry. As the Roundhead column arrived at the square, the crowd was ordered to fall back, creating a wide area before the market stalls where the general could make his address. Fairfax brought his horse to rest and observed the scene from his saddle. When the squeals and murmurs of the crowd subsided, he began.

He told those who could hear that his mercy towards them was honest and in good faith. Only delinquents who continued to bear arms would be dealt with harshly. The populace should go about its normal business, offering service to the occupying soldiers if it was needed. As he said these things, the crowd stared at him in wonder, as if he were a divine being from a far-off magical realm called London.

Having pacified the townsfolk, Fairfax rode the short distance to the wharf. Fisherwomen were gutting the day's catch and men were dragging barrels of pilchard onto dry land. The general was handed a telescope. He looked out into the bustling harbour, saw to the far left of the approaches the smaller castle of St Mawes. Pendennis Castle, which sat opposite, was obscured by masts and rigging from a cluster of tall ships moored in the shallows.

'The mouth of it will need to be tempered,' Fairfax said, indicating the harbour entrance.

'Ten or so ships should do the trick, sire,' said Colonel Fortescue. Fairfax gently nodded and handed the scope to Fortescue as if a nagging problem had finally been solved.

*

The troop marched on, following the winding thoroughfare which in turn led to the castle road; past ale houses and stinking fishmongers wedged along the lapping harbour waters; past vendors and drunkards who had collapsed in the slippery alleyways. Then the long column passed the bend near the small church before the narrow road evened itself into boggy green land. Another scout galloped towards Parliament's foremost general.

'Sire, the Royalist garrison has set flame to Arwenack House.'

Fairfax dug in his heels and cantered towards the building, seeing for the first time the magnificent manor house that looked out onto the mouth of the harbour and which had been marked as a headquarters for the occupying army. In the distance, Fairfax's advance troops were chasing members of the Pendennis garrison up the steep climb towards the castle. Blasts of carbine could be heard as well as the desperate shrieks of the fallen.

Fairfax dismounted. The fire was blazing in the manor's west wing. His men had arrived just in time. He looked on as soldiers carried pails of harbour water to the scene, drenching the flames before they were able to spread further.

'Another hour and we would have been too late!' Fortescue said.

'I sense the governor's hand in this,' said Fairfax. His officers gathered round him as the fiery stack began to smoulder and troops began sifting through Royalist debris.

'The road ahead to the castle has been cleared, sire,' said Fortescue. 'All stragglers have been dealt with. Shall we prepare for siege?'

Fairfax considered this. As much as he would like to make the old governor pay for his treachery, he kept an even temper.

'Not yet,' he said. 'I will allow Governor Arundell some time to reflect on his actions before offering terms of surrender. Only when I have received the old man's answer and taken the rub of him shall we make our move.'

(iii)

After the uncertainty and trepidation of Fairfax's entry, the atmosphere in the market square changed. It seemed that the inhabitants of the town were not, after all, about to experience the terrors of brutal occupation. The opposite seemed to be true. Young Roundhead soldiers moved amongst the crowd, casually speaking with old men and women, showing off their muskets to children, flirting with the young maidens who were scouring the stalls for a cheap cut. One even took a liking to Bethsany's chickens. He haggled with her over a price, quipping with Maben that a soldier's life was best of all.

'You'd do your mother proud serving Parliament's army,' the soldier said. Maben squirmed under the young man's gaze, clinging to Bethsany's sturdy legs. The soldier, unsure about this silent boy, graced Bethsany's palm with a coin. He left with the chicken hanging from his bandolier.

As the crowd thinned and the day grew cold, Bethsany and Maben packed their wares and began the slow walk home. The boy carried the rolled blanket, skipping up the steep hill; Bethsany, weighed down with unsold goods, trudged behind at a distance. A little over half-way from the hill's crest, Bethsany called out. Maben turned and ran back to where she stood. She indicated another, much narrower, road to their right, which led to an old stone cottage.

Bethsany had brought Maben to this place before and the memory of it disturbed him. He grew anxious as Bethsany ordered him inside, refusing at first, screwing up his face in a determined effort to show his displeasure. Bethsany, though, insisted, and scolded him for his disobedience. Eventually she took a tight hold of Maben's arm and pulled him in the direction of the cottage's front door.

She didn't hesitate to enter the place without warning, pushing open the door with a brusque slap of her palm.

Inside, a thin, elderly woman was sitting beside a hearth. Her wispy tufts of hair were pure white, her spindly legs encased in thick stockings. On the floor before her sat a girl eating fish and bread from a wooden bowl. The girl looked up. She had the same barnyard hair as Maben, though it was longer and in places matted; she also had the same pale skin, though a bruise could be seen on her neck. Maben looked at her with a suspicious eye, as if trying to recall a previous uncomfortable encounter. He turned to Bethsany who merely nodded in the girl's direction, encouraging him to make the girl's acquaintance. Reluctantly, Maben edged towards her. He watched the girl scoop fish from the bowl, then push the broiled flakes into her greasy mouth. Her eyes were darkly ringed, as though someone had smudged dirt around them. Her woollen jerkin was caked with muck, her long skirt and ankle boots torn at the seams.

He sat down opposite her. The elderly woman passed him a bowl. Bethsany pulled from her bag a chicken she had withheld from sale. The old woman took it and placed it on a lobster pot next to her which she used as a table. She then poured a cup of strong ale for Bethsany who thanked her; she sat for a while, cradling the cup in her large, work-ravaged hands.

No more words passed between her and the elderly woman. Indeed, no words passed between Maben and the girl. They sat eating their bread and fish, occasionally looking at one another. If Maben had been able to speak in a coherent manner and ask who the girl was, he would have been surprised to learn that she was his twin sister. It had been nine years since the twins' parents had drowned, nine years since Ann and Bethsany had taken the boy and the old woman and her husband had taken the girl. Now that her husband had died and she had slipped into ill-health, she was dependent on the girl to run her errands. Bethsany offered the woman charity on market day when she could.

Maben soon grew irritable. He had eaten the contents of his bowl and wanted to explore. He did so without comment from Bethsany, darting out of the front door and making his way to the rear of the house and into an overgrown garden that reminded him of the forest.

He stood in the long grass, chasing out the bugs and flies that lived there, cupping them in his hand. He examined each one, taking in the delicate structures of their wings, the other-worldly proptosis of their eyes, the dazzling colours of their bodies and legs. Maben wondered what it would be like to fly between the tall grass, imagined himself climbing the tallest tree in the forest and spreading his arms, then sweeping through the air in the manner of a damsel fly. Beetles were his favourite. He found one hidden beneath a rock – as big as a small stone and shiny black in his hand, its shell magically refashioning itself into a dark streak of blue. It sat obediently in his hand, its long antenna probing. Maben decided he would take it home. He would keep it as a pet, and house it in the empty dwelling of Elowen's grandmother, visiting it each day.

The girl stared for a long time. For a moment he seemed to understand their relationship, was able to acknowledge that she was as much part of him as Ann, Bethsany and Elowen. The girl stood and stared for a long time – so long that Maben extended his palm so that she was able to fully appreciate the creature he'd discovered. The girl smiled, revealing blackened teeth, and gently touched the beetle's shell with her finger. Maben did the same, careful not to press too hard lest the greater force caused the beetle pain. Ann had once explained to him how great a person was in relation to the small things that inhabited God's earth. The girl reached out, aligning her palm with Maben's, and the beetle was shunted from the plateau of one to the other. The girl smiled, her teeth, Maben noticed, chipped in certain places. She took hold of the beetle between her forefinger and thumb – lifted it above her head as Maben looked on. He gazed at the creature's underside, giggled as the spindly legs stretched themselves in the air. Then the girl lowered her hand until the beetle was above her eyes. She closed them and opened wide her mouth – and promptly dropped the creature in. She began to chew, splintering the shell, until a dark yellow pus began to dribble onto her lips. Maben cried out – the same high-pitched cry that he made when the footman had come into view. He turned and ran, ran through the tall grass into the cottage, his sister's laughter ringing in his ears.

(iv)

Colonel Richard Fortescue sat alone in the dining room of Arwenack House. Two days had passed since Fairfax's triumphal entry into Falmouth and for the first time in many weeks the colonel was at last able to enjoy a decent meal. Soldiers of his foot regiment had been allowed the run of the town, billeting themselves in the damp, dingy cottages that edged the harbour. Apart from the usual instances of drunkenness and rowdyism, the population of Falmouth town remained pliant, with no sign of an uprising. All that was left to do was to flush out the garrison of Pendennis

Castle. Then, the south-west of England would firmly be under Parliament's control.

As he chewed on boiled cabbage and a tender end of beef, Fortescue found himself unable to fully appreciate the great swathes of territory claimed by the New Model Army. His appetite for war was waning. He knew that great victories were quickly overturned; that the country lurched, at greater cost, first one way then the other as Royalists took back what Parliament had gained. Perhaps, he thought, it was Cornwall that was dampening his outlook. Since his arrival he'd harboured a bad feeling about the place. The weather was too changeable, the population too untrustworthy. More used to life in the city, Fortescue found that the incessant twanging of bowlines and flapping of canvas from ships moored in the harbour played on his nerves. There was an aura of the supernatural, too, that he, a Presbyterian, did not care for. And he found the language of the locals insufferable: an indecipherable mixture of old Cornish and what could only be termed as rough, bawdy English; a language that was good for no man's ears.

There was a knock at the door. Fortescue bade entry. A young orderly entered carrying fresh logs, ready to stoke the fire and clear the table.

'What news of the general?' said Fortescue.

'He's dictating terms, sire. Then he wishes to sleep.'

Fortescue watched the boy go about his business with the plates. 'Tell him I too will soon a-bed, so I am able to rise with the first crow.'

The young orderly gave an ungainly bow and left the

room. Fortescue, despite having eaten, felt cold. He moved from the table to a wainscot chair near the window where he sat drinking port and gazing at the harbour approaches.

Shortly after their arrival at Arwenack House, Fairfax had been taken ill, tiredness and a sharp pain below his ribs causing him distress. The air in the manor, made nauseous by the fire, was deemed by a doctor as the likely cause of his drowsiness, though Fairfax contended this, saying both ailments had reared themselves after the battle at Launceston. The doctor prodded and probed, shook his head. Medicine was dispensed and sleep suggested as remedy. Fairfax, though, continued dictating the terms of Pendennis Castle's surrender from his bed, terms that Fortescue was obliged to present to the governor the next day.

As he sipped his wine, Fortescue considered the general's ill-health to be a signal – a signal that Cornwall and its pagan ways offered nothing but bad luck. Swift victories, he feared, were at an end. An angry, godless wind seemed to be blowing them asunder.

*

At dawn, Fortescue made his way to the manor's courtyard where a small troop of soldiers, stable boys and horses were waiting. The group rode the short distance up the steep hill road from Arwenack House, passing the heavy canons that had been put in place, and on towards the castle's moated entrance, halting before they came into view of Royalist soldiers manning the high wall. A scout was sent ahead, carrying the regimental flag. He informed the guards on the castle's battlements that Corporal Richard Fortescue of the New Model Army wished his presence to be relayed to the governor. The scout also demanded safe passage for the colonel and his men.

Once an agreement had been reached, Fortescue and the others moved on, holding their horses steady before the gate. Inside, the lieutenant governor of Pendennis, Richard Arundell, roused his father in his bed with news that a meeting was to be had. Sir John, more irritable than usual, snorted at this unwelcome intrusion and ordered his son to represent him, adding for good measure that he expected the lieutenant governor to don full military uniform before coming face to face with any traitorous Parliamentary officer. Richard Arundell snarled as he made his way to his quarters to be dressed, angry not at the prospect of speaking with Fortescue but at his father's petty whims.

After much waiting (which Fortescue deemed a slight), the castle gates were opened, and Richard Arundell walked across the drawbridge. Fortescue dismounted and the two men stood at a distance from one another in the gathering light. Each imparted his name and rank, taking good measure of the other as they did so.

Fortescue was handed a roll of sealed parchment which he held up for the younger Arundell to see.

'I have been ordered to deliver, on behalf of General Fairfax, terms of surrender for the garrison at Pendennis Castle.'

'I know precisely what you have come to deliver, sir,' said Richard Arundell.

Fortescue took a pace forward and held out the parchment. Richard Arundell ordered one of the soldiers to retrieve it, as if the thing would sully his hands.

'I assure you, they are generous terms,' said the Colonel with a sharper edge. 'Mark, they might not be as generous next time.'

'I do not doubt it,' said Richard Arundell. 'But my father is a proud man whose loyalty is to the king. Surrender does not come naturally to him. The decision rests in his hands.'

A moment passed with only the gentle lap of waves and the clink of a horse's harness acting as a steady hand between the two groups of men. Under different circumstances, Richard Arundell and Fortescue might have been friends. They were of similar age and stock, each blessed with good prospects. Yet now they stood eye to eye, errand boys in a war they neither wished for nor fully understood.

'Let us hope then, for the sake of the souls who live behind the castle walls, your father's decision proves the correct one,' said Fortescue.

'My father,' said Richard Arundell, 'is in the twilight of his days. His only wish is that his honour will not be blemished through surrender. He would rather find himself buried beneath these castle walls than commit treason.'

Was the younger Arundell wavering? Or hinting, perhaps, that his and his father's hearts were not fully aligned? Fortescue wasn't sure. He briefly wondered whether he should engage with the lieutenant governor on more equitable terms. But he found that he was unable to do so; the imperative of war seemed to be pushing him hard in another direction.

'If, sir,' he said, 'the terms of surrender are rejected, perhaps your father will have his way.'

Fortescue remounted while Arundell, again disappointed

with Fortescue's abrupt manner, stood his ground.

'There are good soldiers in this place, sir,' he said, 'with plenty of powder and shot to see us through. Do not underestimate our conviction. It would be a grave mistake.'

'Your castle is a prison!' shouted the Colonel. 'If our canon does not do the job in hand, your empty bellies will!'

Fortescue pulled on his reins, bringing his animal round, and beckoned his men retreat. Richard Arundell walked across the moat's bridge and gave the order for the portcullis to be lowered. He had not disclosed the ace up his father's sleeve: a mercenary army from across the channel which, with God's speed, might even now be on its way.

9.

(i)

A sharp knock on the cabin door roused the captain of the *Adventurer* from his sleep. Dan Arent, his throat dry, his mouth still bitter from rum and a bad dream, called out, inviting the visitor to enter. A deckhand looked in and informed him that the ship was nearing Cornish waters. Arent nodded and waved the deck boy away. Normally Cadwaller would be the one to convey such a message. Not now; not after their strained discussion of the previous day.

Arent took a wet flannel and washed his face and neck. Then, having dressed, he pondered over the map awhile before making his way onto deck. Cadwaller was at the wheel, a position he'd kept throughout the night. The wind was fair and the ocean calm. The rush of fresh sea air invigorated Arent's mood.

'Best get some sleep, old sailor', Arent said with a grin. 'We'll lie low for a while – take stock before we show our colours, eh?' Cadwaller, his hands fixed firmly to the wheel, said nothing. Arent had no wish to see their friendship deteriorate in such a manner, but he felt affronted by Cadwaller's stubbornness, as well as his friend's easy insistence that Arent remained ungrateful for the help he had received.

'Wheel locked. Preparing hand over,' Cadwaller said and let his hands fall to his side. Arent moved into position and took hold.

'Look, enough of the formalities, I want to …'

'She's all yours,' said Cadwaller, cutting Arent short. Then, with a bitter edge, he added, 'Captain.'

After an hour or so at the wheel, Arent ordered the mainsail to be slackened. The *Adventurer* quickly lost speed, moving forward at a gentle pace, powered by the fore mast alone. It was one o'clock in the afternoon. Dusk, he thought, would be the optimum time to drop anchor. Once at rest, and with the castle in sight, Arent planned on a few hours wait before choosing his moment. Then, there would be no time to spare. As soon as the garrison's vessels had drawn alongside, the *Adventurer's* cargo would be loaded: gunpowder, bullet and match first; foodstuffs and general supplies to follow. And when the hull had been cleared, Arent would turn the *Adventurer* on her tail and head home.

As well as orders to deliver military and stock supplies, Pindar had given Arent a letter addressed to the governor, Sir John Arundell. The contents of the letter, of course, remained unknown to Arent but he surmised it contained instructions regarding the castle's defences, or perhaps arrangements for the future transportation of soldiers. Whatever secrets the letter carried, Arent wasn't interested. He'd placed it in his leather knapsack for safe keeping. At the earliest opportunity he would hand it over to one of the castle's senior officers and be done with it.

By late afternoon, sailing tight to shore, Arent sighted St

Mawes. He ordered the anchor dropped, giving time for the crew to take up their positions.

'Captain! I can see Pendennis!' the boy who sat in the crow's nest shouted. A cheer broke out, which Arent quickly muted.

'What mood is she in?' he asked the boy.

'Angry, Captain – like a devil's head, so's I reckon.'

Cadwaller came on deck. His mood seemed more even than earlier, eager for the job at hand to be set in motion.

'Orders, Captain?' Arent looked at his friend, saw grey, steely eyes, hardened by a new-found anger.

'To the prow – and prepare the beacon. Tell me everything you see.'

At six pm, with only light traffic passing their way, Arent called for the anchor to be raised. The day was fading now; a grim early evening haze was descending on the back of a bitter squall. Arent cut a course eastward, away from the castle. Once the beacon's message had been answered, he would make a decisive tack west, ready to meet the castle's skiff. What's more, their slow passage east would give him time to observe the harbour's entrance and any suspicious movement therein.

The ship padded through choppier waters. As the full extent of the harbour came into view, Arent grew more confident. He could see nothing to cause concern, leading him to believe that Fairfax's army was still days away from Falmouth or, better still, had met fierce resistance elsewhere.

So quiet was it that Arent told Cadwaller to give up the signal to the castle's men. A number of the garrison's soldiers had already spied the *Adventurer* and were grouped on shore, preparing to meet Arent's ship. Cadwaller lit an oil lamp while another crew member shielded the glass with a leather apron. They set the lamp into position on the gunwale and Cadwaller's mate lifted and dropped the apron three times. Then they waited, staring high up at the darkening isthmus, until the soldiers who manned the turrets returned the signal in kind. Now Arent decided to abandon all caution and cut west. He shouted the order; the mainsail flashed out and the timbers and cordage groaned as the ship slowly changed course. Soon they saw the garrison's troops busying themselves along the shoreline, shadowy figures darting like sea flies. Arent gripped the wheel.

'Steady now!' he shouted. 'Make ready with the fore.'

The *Adventurer* drifted in a close haul to a position in line with the castle's beacon. Tighter, tighter they sailed until they neared the shallows beyond which lay the rough jagged rock that could tear the hull of any vessel. Cadwaller, hanging over the side, monitoring the depth, gave a shout; Arent ordered the anchors be dropped. The *Adventurer* dragged to a halt.

Arent's men began preparing the cargo for offloading, hauling the barrels from the hold. Arent looked on as his crew went through their paces, each man taking his position in the chain, the barrels appearing on deck in an instant. He could see the garrison's skiff making good progress; soon it would be alongside, and the job would be done. Then a hard sail home to where a new life beckoned.

'You were expected a time ago!' shouted one of the castle soldiers as the skiff neared. 'A day since.'

Arent and other members of his crew hung over the gunwale as the smaller boat was tethered. The captain had no desire to waste valuable time explaining the late arrival of the gunpowder. Instead, his crew took up a new formation as the first barrels were brought up and secured to the pulleys.

The castle's soldiers waited in anticipation as the first barrel swung precariously above them. Cadwaller muscled his way forward and helped take up the strain, barking at the crew to release the rope as slowly as they were able, all the while marking the tension and speed of the barrel's descent. Arent looked on in silence; transferring Pindar's cargo was going to take longer than he anticipated.

As they began to gain momentum and the third barrel was eased onto the skiff, Arent was alerted by flickers of firelight. It came from amongst the trees that covered the headland below the castle. For some reason the firelight disturbed him. He turned and looked at the smaller castle, St Mawes, as if fearing this new fire was acting as a beacon, communicating some undefined message, but he saw nothing untoward.

It was only after the tenth barrel of powder had been lowered that Arent saw the dark imposing shape of a man-o'-war appear from off the *Adventurer's* stern, pushing through the water like the avenging monster he had seen in his dreams, intent on his punishment.

(ii)

A shot rang out – the unmistakable sound of canon – aimed in the direction of the men gathered on the shoreline. Arent heard screams, watched shadows scuttle across rocks. The shoreline beacon was quickly extinguished. Then another blast, this time from off the *Adventurer's* bow. The shot landed away on the starboard side but close enough to the castle's soldiers for panic to set in. The *Adventurer's* pulley ropes suddenly loosened; two barrels of powder fell into the sea.

'Trim the sails!' Arent yelled and once again began the slow groaning process of readying the pear-shaped vessel to tack, first west, then south.

He spun the ship's wheel, feeling a wave of anxiety surge through him as he glanced at the mizzen, realising that two frigates had emerged in a co-ordinated pincer movement. Arent again gave the order to set the fore and main, willing the wind to punch into the sails. As he did so, more shots pierced the gathering dusk. The second frigate, making its way out of the harbour, now began attacking the garrison while the man-o'-war launched another round in the direction of the *Adventurer*. This time the shot landed closer than the last.

Arent screamed for the ship to pick up speed so they could escape the same way they arrived, but the windward chaser was gaining. Another shot whistled overhead; Arent realised that both ships were now firing at the *Adventurer*. As the fear and chaos of the moment began to grow, Arent cursed himself. His foolishness had done for them all; he should have waited – should have sent a tender into the harbour to cast a fuller eye. Suddenly he realised the true nature of the situation: Fairfax's army had already taken the town, were even now securing the most south westerly coast. How stupid of him to be so hasty, to believe in Pindar's faulty intelligence, to think that fate had for once dealt him a fair hand!

'They're gaining!' shouted Cadwaller. 'We're not going to bring her up to speed!'

It was true. The squall had passed, the wind was light and even. Another two blasts rang out, both landing so close Arent felt the rush in the atmosphere as the shots broke water. The two enemy ships were now on course to cut off the *Adventurer* from the open sea. Arent knew he had a decision to make. He could press on and try to escape, risking the scuttling of his ship, or else surrender and keep the *Adventurer* intact, trading his knowledge of Pindar's network of Royalist sympathisers for a more lenient outcome. The proximity of the next shot, whistling close to the mainsail, made his decision for him. Arent shouted to drop anchor.

Cadwaller, hunkering beneath the prow, called out: 'Has the captain turned into a madman?'

Arent ignored him. He took off his jacket and blouse and tied his shirt to a broom handle. Defiantly, he crossed to the starboard side of the ship and began waving the white cloth at the approaching vessel. Then he crossed to the port side and repeated the action. The second vessel was closing rapidly. Arent could see a group of soldiers standing on the prow, eager to come on board.

Cadwaller ran towards Arent and knocked the broom from his hands. Arent retaliated, the two men clinging to one another like angry, love-torn schoolboys.

'Why have you surrendered, cur?' Cadwaller screamed. 'Have you no shame!' Arent pushed Cadwaller against the gunwale.

'These men will not die on my account, Cadwaller ... They

will not be sacrificed for a deposed and wretched English king!'

The struggle continued, the culmination of hours of bitterness, but it was a mere side show as Arent's hapless crew looked on at the two vessels edging alongside. As the first Parliamentary soldiers jumped onto the *Adventurer's* deck, Arent and Cadwaller were forcibly parted. The officer in charge called out for the captain of the ship to make himself known. Naked from the waist up, his torso red after the struggle with his second-in-command, Arent, wiping blood from his lip, declared himself the owner and commander, which proved something of a surprise to his captors, who looked upon him in his mussed and shabby state with considerable unease.

10.

(i)

The two parliamentary frigates guided the *Adventurer* into Falmouth Harbour. Dan Arent, Cadwaller Jones and the rest of the crew had been placed cross-legged, wrists tied, in the ship's hold, with musket barrels trained on them by three nervous looking soldiers.

'They look barely old enough to wipe their own arses,' said Cadwaller. The remark was directed at Arent who was sitting beside his deputy. He did not reply but felt pleased that Cadwaller was at last being sociable again. He just prayed that Cadwaller didn't let his temper get the better of him. The soldiers might be young, but they could pull a trigger as well as any man.

Arent surveyed his crew. Humiliated, frightened, some finding the act of breathing difficult in the dark and damp. It would take all his skills to negotiate clemency. Pindar had recounted to him the brutality of the Parliamentarian army. And yet the outline of a plan began to form, a plan that he hoped might win his crew their freedom.

During the first hour of the *Adventurer's* capture, troops had searched the captain's quarters in Arent's presence and confiscated maps and documents from a sea chest that lay therein – intelligence that would be passed on to Fairfax's officers for further examination. But Dan Arent knew his papers contained little information of any worth. His contacts in Rotterdam remained hidden, although it would be a mistake for him to take the Parliamentarians for fools. Pindar's name would, he was certain, surface soon enough. No, the best chance of their release was the letter from Pindar addressed to the governor of Pendennis Castle, Sir John Arundell. During the initial search, Arent had watched as a soldier spilled out the contents of his knapsack onto the captain's table, shaking the bag for all it was worth.

'Those are my personal possessions,' said Arent. 'Possessions of great sentimental value.' The soldier looked at the comb, scissors, knife, flannel and other items with interest. 'They were given to me by my late wife. I would appreciate it if they remained with me.' The soldier held the knife, weighed it admiringly in his hand. 'Sir?' An older Roundhead stepped forward. He too perused the objects, looking every now and again at the captured owner of the ship. Much to the younger soldier's delight, he said: 'Take the knife for yourself, lad, 'n' leave the rest.' Thereafter the bag remained in Arent's quarters, the untouched letter secreted in its pocket.

As the boats drifted towards harbour, the prisoners were brought up on deck. A crowd had formed on the wharf as if preparing to welcome home a group of long-lost sailors. But as the ships neared, Arent was able to take in the faces of these people – uncertain, frightened faces, scared of what the present and future held in store.

The ships dropped anchor and smaller boats came alongside to ferry Arent's men to land. Amongst the crowd a cohort of soldiers appeared, driving the onlookers to the side. They stood with muskets ready.

'These bastards certainly know how to make a working chap feel welcome,' said Cadwaller.

'Let's take things easy,' said Arent. 'Do as they say and no backchat. We're merchant sailors – nothing more, nothing less. We're not here to fight.'

Cadwaller snorted. 'They can knock seven bells out of one another for all I care. I've no interest in their rotten king or their rotten parliament. I'll tell 'em so, an' all.'

Once the *Adventurer*'s crew were assembled on the wharf, they were taken at gun point to the market square. The folk milling about gave the prisoners a wide birth, speaking in hushed tones as they passed by. Arent saw this as a disturbing sign. He looked for evidence of timbers to fashion a scaffold but saw nothing, only old men and women selling their wares: fish and scrawny scraps of bloody game, trussed up over dirty squares of hessian, waiting to be sold.

They were led to a stone building – the old town gaol that dated from medieval times. Before they entered, they were split into two groups. The first group was led inside and incarcerated in one of two cells that lay below ground. The second group, comprising Arent, Cadwaller and seven other crew members, followed. Arent baulked when he saw the spartan conditions in which they were to be held.

'This is intolerable!' Arent said to the commanding officer. 'I demand to see your superior.'

The officer looked at Arent with barely hidden contempt. 'Men who are in league with traitors should be glad of the most basic facility, I reckon,' he said.

'My men require water. And food. Do you expect the absence of disease and death in this place? Disease spreads, sir. And it spreads easily beyond the confines of a filthy cell such as this.'

The officer ordered Arent quiet. 'I will arrange the provision of sustenance for your men. You can expect a trial during which your fate will be determined. Until then you are in the hands of your God and England's Parliament.'

A small grille, situated at ground level, was the only source of natural light in the dungeons. Two wooden pails for each cell were brought in by soldiers to act as latrines. Later, the door of Arent's cell was opened and another pail, filled with fresh water, was set down. The officer in charge, who Arent had spoken with earlier, appeared in the doorway and said: 'We are not barbarians, as you seem to think, Captain Arent. The pails will be emptied and re-filled tomorrow so I advise you to use your resources wisely.'

The door slammed shut and a long silence ensued, broken by Cadwaller. 'Well, let's not get disheartened lads. Let's think of it as a holiday. It's a shame I haven't got my penny whistle – that would've cheered you all up no end.'

There were chuckles of laughter. Cadwaller's penny whistle had been a source of irritation for many a good year. A shout came from the cell next door. 'There'd be no need for the gallows if you'd brought it, Cadwaller. We'd have done ourselves in within the hour!'

The laughter continued, eventually petering away to silence as each man reflected on the situation at hand. How many days and nights were they expected to remain here? A cold brick floor to sleep on, a small patch of light to admire, their anxieties building at the thought of hanging or worse. Arent considered all these things – also the fact that he had been deprived of his livelihood. The *Adventurer* would be scuttled, he was sure, or else taken by Parliament and re-fitted for their navy. For a brief harrowing moment, he saw only years of poverty and hardship ahead of him. But such thoughts eventually worked to steel his resolve. If they survived this trial, he determined to work his passage to the East Indies. Pindar's half money lay waiting for him in his rooms in Rotterdam, his final, lasting hope to sail to the new world he craved.

(ii)

Following his meeting with his twin sister, Maben's demeanour changed. He was no longer the carefree boy who had been touched by the moon. Now he became a sullen-faced scamp who resented his God-fearing wards. At prayer meetings, hosted by members of Ann's church, he screwed up his face, causing Bethsany to prod his arm. And when he carried out his chores he did so in a languid, slovenly way that was more in keeping with a whipped cur than a boy who was filled with the grace of the lord.

'What ails you, Maben?' Ann asked him but received no indication of an answer. Bethsany was sharper – she snarled at his behaviour. Ann remained unaware of Bethsany's secret trips to see the elderly woman who had taken on the role of ward to the second twin. And so she decided that Elowen's departure was the root cause of Maben's displeasure, a displeasure that existed to a greater extent than she realised.

One afternoon she gave Maben a basket of bread, eggs and barley cakes to take to Old Elijah. It was April now and the weather changed at will. Within a minute, white clouds blessed by the sun would suddenly part, revealing murky grey landscapes of sky. It had been so today; Ann looked out and saw the bright morning sunshine readying itself to be replaced by dark squalls of rain.

'Be quick,' she said to him, 'lest thunder condemns us to an afternoon inside.'

She watched as Maben trudged over the grassland and crossed the threshold of the forest, entering without so much as a farewell glance or a wave. She hoped a visit to Old Elijah might change the boy's sullen mood. An hour or so in male company would do him good.

Maben, infused with new darker tricks, decided he was going to negotiate a different path. He did not skip long in the direction of Old Elijah's dwelling. Instead, he crouched behind a tree and spied on Mistress Ann, waiting for her to turn and go back inside, safe in the false knowledge that he had been sent on his way. When she at last disappeared, the boy took the opposite track in the direction of the hillock where the footman was buried, veering off to visit that place where Elowen had buried the wooden chest. Maben had dreamed of inserting the small key into the brass lock, lifting the lid, and gazing upon the treasures therein. In his dreams, the chest had been a portal to strange worlds of darkness and light – a rabbit hole into which he could crawl, emerging, perhaps, into a golden forest populated by tame beasts and fat juicy birds.

The boy had difficulty recalling the precise tree which marked the spot where the chest was buried. He knelt beside an oak, scratched at the moist earth, decided no, this was not where they had dug after all. Elowen had taught him the names of trees but his interest in their names did not hold. Now he set down Old Elijah's basket of eggs, bread and cakes and walked aimlessly from oak to elm, staring absently at branches, roots and trunks, trying to gauge where the chest was hidden. At last, he fell upon it. A gnarled root acted as a marker – he remembered that Elowen had told him so. Maben's excitement extended itself into a shibboleth of sound: hoots and mumblings of joy as he clawed the earth, anticipating the sight of the wooden lid branded with three feathers. Concentrating on his digging, he failed to notice the presence of two people – one who was a man standing at a distance, and a girl who stood closer, so close she could have leaned herself forward and tapped him on his shoulder.

He looked up, astonished. His twin sister was standing beside him, staring in that discomforting, all-knowing way she had stared at him before. Even though the man was some way off, Maben was able to take the measure of him: tall, hunched, with straggly black hair. He wore a long black coat, black stockings and sharp buckled shoes; a large felt hat obscured his face, giving him a sinister, otherworldly look that seemed to ice the mellow forest's atmosphere. Maben looked round; the trees seemed to be closing in. And it had darkened, as if the branches had bowed themselves slightly in order to conceal the light.

The girl turned away and began to walk in the direction of the obscured man. She beckoned Maben to follow her. No longer was he thinking of the buried wooden chest with its brass lock and mystical gateways to a land of ripe adventure. The girl was now his guide – a mirror image who cast a spell, leading him to his rightful place. Maben stood as if in a trance and walked after her – not in the direction of the dead footman, not in the direction of Old Elijah's dwelling, but along a trackway never before seen; a secret trackway, known only to the dark figure, which led to the castle.

11.

(i)

When the church bells rang for evening prayer and Maben had still not returned, Ann Netherton put on her heavy cloak and walked across the grasslands to Old Elijah's dwelling. He was dozing and woke with a start at her call. Ann entered to discover him lying on his soiled bed along with dogs, cats and chickens – all sheltering from the dark clouds and the sudden spit of rain.

'Where is the boy Maben?' she asked.

Old Elijah sat up and rubbed his rheumy eyes. 'I hasn't seen thar boy, Mistress Ann. Then again, I's been sleeping, so I ain't seen much at all.'

'I sent him with a basket for you – eggs, cakes, bread …'

'Cider's the only meal I's had today, Mistress,' he said with a grin.

Ann looked around for evidence that Maben had completed his journey, cursing Old Elijah for his sinfulness and dependence on drink as she did so.

'Mistress Ann,' the old man said. ''E's a good lad, young Maben is. ''E's checkin' Elowen's traps, is where 'e is.'

'Let us hope in the Lord's name you are right,' said Ann

111

and, with a final look of disdain, promptly left Old Elijah's dwelling.

Her greatest fear was that Maben had been snatched by Fairfax's soldiers. The thought was a disturbing one. The boy was no soldier – he would perish within a week. Then she considered his recent moodiness, his disruptive behaviour, which she had looked upon as nothing but a deep yearning for Elowen. Had he, she wondered, in his despair at not seeing her, made his way to seek her out?

Ann began to scour the forest. First, she followed the route between the trees where she had last seen the boy. She discovered nothing untoward; then she turned and followed another loose trackway in the direction of the road which led to town. Ann always felt uncomfortable in the forest. It was a realm she associated with pagan worship, a place of danger and misrule. Elowen's grandmother, when she was young and able, would spend her time wandering among the trees, making offerings to the false gods that she said drifted like spirits all around. Ann had told Maben that such beliefs were the mark of the devil. And yet these beliefs had been passed down to Elowen. Had the boy, she wondered, succumbed to this blasphemy?

She stopped. In the distance, lying beside a gnarled oak, lay the basket she had handed to him that morning. Ann hurried over, faltering as she stood before it. Scraps of cake, bread and broken eggs were scattered about, as if something or someone had scavenged until its heart was content.

'Maben! Maben!' she called out, her words echoing faintly through the trees. The boy was in danger, of that she was certain. She ran back to her dwelling, hopeful that Bethsany had news, but fearful, too, of what she might be told.

(ii)

On the third day of their incarceration, shortly after dawn, the crew of the *Adventurer* were awakened by the sound of a key turning in the cell door. It opened; an officer of the New Model Army entered.

'Captain Arent?' he asked, looking around the dark, stinking cell.

Arent yawned and replied, 'I am he.'

The officer took a moment to weigh up the dishevelled man sprawled on the hard stone floor. 'You are to accompany me to army headquarters. Make yourself ready.'

Arent struggled to a standing position and, once upright, surveyed the faces of his men. Some looked at him with fear in their eyes; others remained as they were, either laid out on the floor or crouched with their heads pressed to their knees. Cadwaller was sitting against a wall, nonchalantly picking dirt from his fingernails.

'God bless you, Captain,' said one of Arent's men. Several others repeated his sentiment.

'While I'm away, Cadwaller will be in command,' Arent said. Cadwaller remained silent. Arent, immediately falling foul of his friend's attitude, was about to demand a response when the officer said, 'Captain – if you will.'

His hands were shackled and he was escorted through the town – past the wharf, past the ale house, past the small church that sat on the edge of a tight bend. Then they took to the straight, in full view of the harbour approaches, to Arwenack Manor where the Dutchman's fate would be sealed.

He was shown to a ground floor room where he stood before what seemed to be a military court consisting of Corporal Fortescue and two other officers sitting behind a desk. One of the men, to Fortescue's right, held a quill in his hand, ready to transcribe Arent's answers to whatever questions the court was about to ask. Arent thought of the letter sitting in his knapsack and prayed that its existence might lessen the severity of his and the crew's punishment. Fortescue sat upright and clasped his hands together in the manner of one who is about to call a room to prayer.

'Name,' he said.

'Dan Arent, captain of the *Adventurer*.'

Fortescue pondered over the answer for a moment as if trying to fully recollect the circumstances under which the *Adventurer* had been brought to harbour. A parchment was pushed across the table. Fortescue read it; satisfied, he looked up.

'Your ship has been impounded and is now under the authority of Parliament,' he said. 'The cargo, comprising food and powder, illegally bound for Pendennis Castle, is also under military jurisdiction.'

Fortescue turned to the officer who was serving as scribe. 'The report, if you please,' he demanded. The man selected a second roll of parchment from several that were piled on the desk and handed it to his commander. Fortescue unfurled it and the officer to Fortescue's left promptly weighted the corners with four horse brasses taken from a satchel. Fortescue continued. 'The report suggests that you willingly surrendered without recourse to violence – which sits well in your favour – whereupon you and your crew were taken to the town gaol. You have remained in gaol these past three nights. Have you anything to say, Captain, before I pass sentence?'

Arent sighed. 'I am a merchant, sir, not a soldier. The *Adventurer* is my livelihood. I take work where I am able.'

'And with whom did you secure this contract to provide powder to Pendennis?'

'I am not able, sir, to give the gentleman's name.'

'He was an emissary for the king, that much is clear.'

'His name, sir, escapes me.'

'Perhaps an indefinite period in gaol will spark your memory.'

Arent began to plead. 'If that is your will, sir, then I am ready to serve punishment. All I ask is that you set free my men. They are poor sailors, nothing more, nothing less.'

Fortescue let Arent's words hang before deciding to conclude the game. 'We are aware of who you have been dealing with,' he said. 'The eyes and ears of the new commonwealth sees and hears far.'

Arent, feeling that his position was weak, was about to make an offer to hand over the letter when Fortescue – eager now, it seemed, for the matter to be closed – said: 'You have lost your ship and your livelihood, Mr Arent. Some would say that is punishment enough.'

'I would concur with that view, sir,' Arent said.

'I'm sure you would. If I said the name Sir Paul Pindar,

perhaps you would do me the courtesy of denying that it was he who arranged your escapade?'

Arent remained silent.

'I will judge your silence, Mr Arent, as the opposite of a denial. Therefore, sir, under the powers granted me by Parliament I see no reason to detain you or your crew any longer. You are free, on condition that you and your men leave England and return to your homeland immediately. A payment of two shillings per man will be made to secure your journey.'

Arent could barely believe his ears. 'I thank you, sir,' he said. 'I thank you.'

'The war that rages in our nation is between Parliament and the king,' said Fortescue. 'It is a war that does not concern you. Let us pray forthwith that it remains so.'

Arent was ushered out of the building. A throng of people was jostling to gain entry, eager to petition Fairfax's representative with an array of concerns. Troops prevented a number of volatile individuals from breaking through the line. As the soldier escorting Arent demanded licence to walk through the crowd, a tall, fair-haired woman wearing a thick black cloak addressed him. 'You, sir,' she said, 'I beg you – allow me to plead my case before your commanding officer.'

The soldier ignored her. In her desperation, the woman turned to Arent. 'Then I beg you, sir. It concerns a child. It is a matter of life and death.'

Arent stopped. 'I am afraid I am unable to help you, lady. It is not my place.'

The woman, though, was insistent. 'But you have access to

Arwenack Manor. Can you not take me in? That is all I ask —
the chance of a hearing with Colonel Fortescue.'

She took hold of his arm now; Arent gently eased himself
away. 'I have no access. I am released from gaol. I shall return
to my men.'

He felt pity for this woman and wondered about her
cause. 'Wait,' said Arent to the soldier who was escorting him.
'Can you not find time to heed this woman's pleas?'

The soldier, irritated by this turn of events, turned to the
woman and shouted: 'Stand back! We must be on our way.
This man is a prisoner under my guard.'

But she insisted. 'I beg you,' she said again to the soldier.
'Tell the officer in charge that Ann Netherton wishes to
speak with him on account of her son. I believe he has taken
to Pendennis Castle of his own volition. Sir, he is a boy of ten
years, timid of mind. He will not survive in such a place.'

The soldier, angered by the woman's continued insistence,
ordered Arent to move along. Ann Netherton stood her
ground. 'Your army is ready to fire ordnance at the castle. Folk
have seen heavy canon moved into position. My son's
temperament is weak. I wish only to petition the commanding
officer to desist — on my life, that is all that I will.'

She turned away, trying desperately to push through the
line of soldiers. The men held firm and refused to let her
through. The crowd began to surge forward, shouting their
grievances. Arent, alarmed that the woman was suddenly
caught up in this melee, attempted to pull her from harm. She
lashed out, scolding him in the name of the Lord for trying to
prevent her right to state her case.

Eventually the soldier escorting Arent jabbed him in the back, away from the crowd. 'Hurry along,' he said. 'We cannot dally here all day.' And so, they walked towards the town gaol, Arent, with sadness in his heart, glancing over his shoulder as Ann Netherton continued her futile attempt to gain entry to Arwenack Manor.

12.

(i)

Newly promoted to the rank of sergeant as a reward for saving the Prince of Wales, Elowen was ordered to oversee night patrols around the castle's perimeter. The soldiers resented her authority. To them she was an insignificant boy named Elijah whose oversized boots, breeches and trench coat were more suited to a jester in a travelling fair. Whatever she'd done as she carried the Prince of Wales' standard to the shoreline, they whispered, didn't warrant promotion of any kind. As she did her rounds of the battlements, to mark that the sentries were fully awake, she was met with uncomfortable silences and deeply suspicious eyes.

Kettleby showed no signs of jealousy regarding Elowen's advancement. His fever had subsided and he was thankful for the support Elowen had given him. In order to show his appreciation, he reconstructed the tiny shelter where they slept. He reinforced the roof with lengths of wood stripped from the stables; the cold uneven floor he covered with matting and hay wrapped in a hessian sheet. Because Elowen patrolled throughout the night, Kettleby did his best to make sure she slept undisturbed during the day. His duties as ensign were limited now; only in the mornings, when Richard

Arundell observed the forming up of the garrison, was Kettleby required to stand to attention holding the castle's flag. Some days Richard Arundell didn't appear at all, the governor's son spending less and less time inspecting the troops as the weeks dragged on. Only very rarely did his father, the governor, old Sir John the Faithful, appear on the parade ground. Most of the time, it was whispered, he remained in his quarters, his nose and cheeks red as field poppies, staring into his brandy cups.

Kettleby filled his day helping the other poor wretches who slept on the parade ground. He entertained the children with stories and demonstrations of his prowess in flag waving as the women struggled to cook the meagre rations that were handed out each morning. Occasionally soldiers returned from day patrol and scolded Kettleby for interfering with their wives. He protested that he had no ill intention towards these women, only wishing to help where he was able. But Kettleby was naïve; he wasn't made to be in a place like this. When he looked to the women to vouch for him and quell their husband's suspicions he was met only with laughter and silence.

Occasionally Kettleby would look into the shelter and settle for a while next to Elowen as she slept. Still wearing her greatcoat, curled up with her back to him, he would reach out to stroke her brown hair then stop himself from doing such a sinful thing. To further show his admiration, he placed the beer, mutton and ends of bread that he'd traded for tobacco in a corner so that Elowen would see the food when she woke. It was important, he told her as he cut up her meat, that she received sustenance before she toured the perimeter walls at night. Elowen looked at him as she ate, remembering to bite hard and drink long in the manner of a boy.

(ii)

Throughout the hours of darkness, Elowen moved along the battlements. Soldiers stood in pairs, at a distance of fifty yards. Watchmen, placed on the castle turret, sought out movement from the direction of the town. Richard Arundell had warned the garrison that Fairfax's army would launch an attack. He predicted it would be a frontal attack but he did not dismiss Parliamentary soldiers attempting to scale the castle's southernmost defences via the rough pathway that wound its way from the sea front, steadily climbing through birch and elm trees and uncertain terrain.

In the early hours, Elowen stood alongside the castle's turret looking out over the postern gate. She could see the forest and the raging sea beyond, lit by the moon, and came to thinking of the strange girl she had seen hiding among the trees. No other soldiers wished to investigate the forest at night. It was a place, they said, given over to vagabonds and worse. They recounted rumours that the devil resided there, a tale harking back to King Henry's day when the castle was built. It was said the devil once sat on the highest point of the headland and was angered when the castle took over his rightful place.

One night, Elowen saw the flickering light of a fire amongst the trees beyond the southern wall. Fearing a Roundhead plot, she asked for volunteers to accompany her onto the sloping headland but none of the soldiers who stood on the battlements dared to follow. Elowen, eager to prove herself, unfurled her slingshot and said she would go by herself. Before she left, she warned that she would report the soldiers' cowardice to Richard Arundell even though they knew full well that she would not do so.

A shadowy night forest held no fear for Elowen. Sometimes, while her grandmother had slept soundly in her bed, she had left the tiny dwelling they shared and wandered among the trees. She knew every trackway, every mound of grass of the forest where she lived, allowing herself to be guided by the moon and stars. It was not so with the headland forest before her now. As she slipped out of the castle's southern gate, she turned and looked up at the great turret framed by a starless night sky, before making her way slowly along the dirt path that ran parallel to the castle wall. The sharp gradient fell away, causing Elowen to steady herself, the soft, spongy earth making it difficult to retain balance. Through the trees, lit only by the bright grey half-moon – a moon that was occasionally impeded by scudding night clouds – she saw the movement of a thousand shadows. The forest seemed to be alive. She stopped and collected several smooth, oval-shaped stones. She placed six in the pocket of her greatcoat and one in the bed of her slingshot before advancing along the narrow descending path with its steep slopes of soil and scree. She caught the smell of wood smoke sweeping towards her like incense on the breeze. It was not coarse or uncomfortable to her senses but sweet and enticing. And then a flickering of light – the flames of a fire – caught her eye mid-point in her descent. She considered this for a moment. Could a single blaze really suggest that a regiment of Fairfax's army was on the march? Elowen was caught in two minds: return to the castle and report what she had seen, or else edge closer to observe the precise nature of the threat that lay before her.

She walked on, the pathway twisting left and then right, so that she ascended before it dropped again into a tight groove. Once more she struggled to secure her footing. The fire was clear now; she could hear the wheeze and snap of fresh logs. And she could see three figures before it, one of whom was dancing an unwieldly jig before the flames.

Elowen stopped. It was Maben who was dancing. Beside him was the raggedy girl she had seen when she escorted the Prince of Wales. The third figure was that of a man, wearing a black coat and hat, seated on a large smooth boulder, reminiscent of a makeshift throne.

'Maben!'

It took a moment or two before Maben saw Elowen. He stopped, as if considering something of great importance, then walked uncertainly towards her. The raggedy girl looked on with an angry, disapproving gaze. Elowen welcomed the boy with open arms. As she gathered Maben towards her, she saw the man turn in her direction. He pushed the brim of his hat with a long, gnarled finger, revealing his face. It was a shrivelled face, studded with welts. His eyes burned red – like a lizard or a snake or some other fearsome creature. Elowen shivered at the sight. Sensing danger, she said, 'Hurry, boy! Let us away from here.'

13.

(i)

The crew of the *Adventurer* were marched to the wharf where a boat lay ready to spirit them to France. As they waited to board, each man was given his two shillings – General Fairfax's leaving gift – to add to their half pay when they returned to Rotterdam.

Arent could see his own ship at anchor in the harbour, the fluyt's barrelled shape distinguishing the vessel from others moored nearby. Before the *Adventurer* left the wharf for its mooring, Arent had been allowed on board to secure his personal possessions. He had gone straight to his quarters and retrieved his knapsack, checking that Pindar's letter had not been stolen. Then he'd been escorted to the gaol where he announced the good news to his men – they were free.

'What did you promise?' Cadwaller asked as they waited to board.

'Only that we'd leave England,' said Arent, 'and not return.'

'What makes 'em think we'd even consider returning to this 'ere shit hole?' Cadwaller said and spat on the ground.

Arent looked downcast. He wished he could have somehow delivered the letter to the castle governor and told

Cadwaller so. His friend, though, was not as conscientious.

'Give it to one of their officers,' he said, 'or one of their regulars. Or better still, tear it up and throw the pieces in the brine – it's not any of our business now.'

Arent was loathe to hand over the letter to Fortescue lest the action complicate their departure. Arent tried to clear his mind of the matter. Perhaps Cadwaller was right; it wasn't any of their business. Let the castle governor make his own decisions. Pindar's message was most probably merely stating what any rational man would consider. Surely, no governor would contemplate enduring a vicious siege when generous terms of surrender were available? What would such vain obstinacy achieve?

It began to rain – fine rain drifting in from the north. Shouts went up from Arent's crew that they'd waited long enough; it seemed to do the trick because a gangplank was now put in place. Arent's men cheered and began to ready themselves with new purpose, their expectations of a safe voyage home evident in their speech and laughter.

'They're preparing to board, Captain,' Cadwaller said. 'The sooner we get out of here the better.'

Arent looked on, trying hard to make sense of his jumbled thoughts. He was thinking of the woman, Ann Netherton, who had pleaded with him outside Arwenack Manor. And he thought of her son, who had embarked on a fool's errand to gain entry to the castle. It was the woman's fear that the boy was entering a charnel house that played most on his mind. Arent had wanted to help – saw in her the same desperation he'd felt when he pictured his wife and children sinking into the channel sea. But he'd been unable to provide the woman with comfort or hope before Fortescue's soldiers pushed her away. Had she been successful in her petition, he wondered? Arent sighed – he doubted it. It was yet another sad tale of injustice and wasted lives. How he'd wanted to tell Ann Netherton that, yes, he too knew the pain of losing a child. And yet, instead of delivering the letter to the castle's governor – a letter that might save the boy – he was in line to board ship, readying himself to run away.

'It's time,' said Cadwaller, tugging at Arent's sleeve. 'In a few hours we'll be in Rotterdam, supping in a tavern, with not a care in the world!'

The rain was coming in heavy, now. Arent stared at his deputy – vacant, unbecoming. 'I cannot,' he said.

'Eh?' said Cadwaller. 'What can't you? Don't tell me you've fallen ill, man?'

'No, I am not ill. I must stay,' he said. 'Go ahead and board ship. My business here remains unfinished.'

Cadwaller drew himself close to his friend. 'You cannot stay, Captain!' he whispered, harsh and bold. 'It is your duty to leave with your men!'

Arent looked about. 'When you return to Rotterdam, go to my room. Pindar's money lies beneath my bed. Pay the men and pay yourself. I am staying, Cadwaller. I cannot fully explain the reasons to you, suffice to say I have made my decision.'

'Is it a woman?' said Cadwaller, all-knowing, reading his friend like a well-worn map. 'Is that what's turning you into an insensible wretch?'

Arent smiled. He should have known; his friend was always able to pick up the faintest scent, find the clearest picture. 'I ask of you one favour. Create a diversion so I can disappear to the market square.' He took hold of Cadwaller's hand. 'We'll meet again when I return home.'

A clap of thunder rumbled from the dark sky. Cadwaller began to laugh. 'You're a fool, Captain. You don't owe this stinking town a thing,' he said.

'Perhaps I am a fool. But that's for me to decide,' said Arent. 'Now, friend, do as I ask.'

'Is that an order?'

Arent smiled. 'Yes, that's an order.'

Cadwaller Jones's reckless nature was well known. When he and Arent fought together in the European wars, his courage and tendency towards the unexpected surprised in equal measure. Cadwaller seemed to have the luck and *nous* of the devil; it was said that if he fell from a bell tower he'd land in a hay wagon. Always first in the charge, always willing to take a risk; so quick witted that his fellow soldiers reckoned he could blather his way to make a firing squad lower their weapons.

Now he moved backwards along the wharf like a man who had supped too much ale. The gangplank had been tied fast and the *Adventurer's* crew were moving forward to board. Cadwaller began to laugh as he mingled with the crew, laughter that became more and more pronounced, catching the attention of the few soldiers tasked with seeing the prisoners leave English soil. Jauntily, he headed in another direction, to the opposite side of the wharf, barging into a brawny crew member known as Irish Tom, accusing the man of being a blind imbecile who needed to watch where he was going. There was no love lost between the two and Cadwaller's words hit their mark: the Irishman took immediate offence. Cadwaller persevered with his baiting, telling the six-footer he had the brains of a wood slug, much to the amusement of those watching on. When Cadwaller began pushing the big fellow, a scuffle broke out with many interventions from other members of the *Adventurer's* crew. Eventually, sodden by rain, irritated by Cadwaller, and tired of the hold-up that prevented them from boarding ship, Irish Tom did exactly what his tormentor hoped he'd do: he took the smaller man by the scruff of his neck and pushed him towards the edge of the wharf.

Even though Irish Tom's anger was high, the push he gave his irritant was not strong enough to propel Cadwaller into the brine. Yet Arent's deputy played the scene for all it was worth; with theatrical gestures worthy of the London stage, he teetered and tottered and feigned imbalance, before falling over the side with a high merry shout. A strange mix of laughter accompanied by disbelief broke out as soldiers and crew members rushed forward. Some leaned over the wharf in an attempt to reach the stricken Cadwaller, whose arms and legs flailed as though a whirlpool had taken hold, while others remonstrated with Irish Tom for his rough temper. Something akin to a melee was soon underway as the *Adventurer's* men took sides, the towering figure of Irish Tom stoutly defending his actions. Arent smiled. With the rain hammering, Fortescue's soldiers in panic, and Cadwaller roiling in the water, the captain of the *Adventurer* took full advantage of the distraction and ran towards the square.

(ii)

Cadwaller disappeared. One moment he was flailing, the next he was gone. The *Adventurer's* crew called out, threw ropes and a casting net which was lying discarded on the wharf. Grappling hooks were used to sweep across the water in the hope that he would surface and take hold. But it was as if something had dragged him under or snagged him in the depths. The mood of the crew turned to anguish; the deep-lying currents in these parts, said a local man shaking his head, were strong and lightening quick. Cadwaller's shipmates scurried to and fro, expecting him to rise up somewhere — anywhere — at any moment, a hopeful expectation that didn't occur.

A captain of Fortescue's troop appeared, eager to discover the reason for the hold up. His bemused soldiers, trying to make sense of what had happened, pushed Irish Tom forward, holding him in check. He was the culprit, they said. His fists had sent the man under. The captain listened to other anxious accounts of what had taken place. Yes, said Arent's men, Cadwaller had riled them all with his merry making but Irish Tom didn't push hard enough to send him spinning off the wharf. Irish Tom said nothing, stood steely-eyed, as if expecting a charge of affray or, worse, murder. But the heavy rain played its part in the proceedings; so too did the angry shouts coming from the frigate docked alongside, the crew eager to cast off and take Arent's men to France.

Suspicious about the altercation and unwilling to spend time worrying about a drunkard who had lost his footing, the captain of troop lined up the *Adventurer's* crew and made a head count. He wasn't surprised to discover that another prisoner apart from Cadwaller was missing. He stared at Arent's men, demanded to know the identity of the absent sailor but was met with shrugs and uncertain looks. All they wanted, they said, was to set sail for home. Fearing that he had been hoodwinked, the commanding officer ordered a small boat to drag the harbour; the other troops he instructed to make an immediate sweep of the market square.

The soldiers went roughly among the stalls, demanding answers from sellers who were sheltering from the downpour as well as the drunkards and sodden children herding hogs. They asked the guards who stood outside the town gaol, the old men loitering by the tavern; they passed the woman Ann Netherton who was sermonising and conducting prayers for the safe return of the mute boy touched by the moon, her small congregation kneeling before her in the hammering rain as she raised her voice to the angry sky, inviting the Lord to show mercy and return the boy to his rightful place. It was clear that Fortescue's soldiers were wasting their time; they turned their attention to the cobbled alleyways that jutted onto the waterfront. Ann watched them from her vantage point in front of the alehouse. When they had disappeared, she whispered to one of the figures before her, a man draped in her thick black cloak.

'Come,' she said. 'We must hurry away before the soldiers return.'

Arent raised himself and fell in beside her, keeping the hooded cloak she had given him pulled tight over his head.

'Where to?' he asked.

'Somewhere safe,' she said. 'Walk quickly to the top of the hill and pray that no Roundheads travel this way.'

Arent did his best but struggled with the steep gradient as they walked from the town, his breath short, his chest tightening with every step. Ann was brisk and confident in her movement, taking long strides as the rising hill took its toll on her companion, her skirt billowing, her loose hair heavy in the rain.

'We must look a strange couple, good wife,' Arent gasped.

'Save the precious breath God gave you,' was her reply. 'And I am no man's "good wife".'

Arent fell silent and concentrated on the task in hand.

At the brow of the hill the captain of the *Adventurer* stopped. Ann berated him.

'This is not the time – a short distance and we will be away from the town. There,' she said, pointing towards a narrow stretch of woodland. 'A concealed pathway will lead us to safety.'

'Forgive me,' said Arent, gasping and holding his chest. 'A minute is all I crave. Go on ahead. I will follow, I promise.'

Ann strode forward, disappearing into a dark tree-lined tunnel that reminded Arent of a fairy tale he once read to his children. The thought gave him new purpose and he stumbled forward. Although this new trackway was another steep climb, it was not as hard going as the great hill they had negotiated from town. Ann's rapid pace slackened now. The track was muddy; her thin boots sank into it, the hem of her long skirt absorbing the worst. By the time Arent saw they were following the line of a stream, his breath settled, became more even.

'Thank you, mistress,' he said, 'for shielding me. If I had been caught, I would have been returned to the town gaol.'

Ann kept her eyes firmly fixed before her.

'There is much injustice in the world, that much I know. You do not look like a delinquent or a dissembler ready for the town gaol. What's more you took pity on me when I was verbally attacked by Fortescue's soldiers. I believe there is good in your heart and that is why I shielded you.'

Her stern efficiency intrigued him. He could see a dwelling ahead, nestling on the far edge of a forest, but she continued following the stream. Then, once the trackway curved, he saw a second dwelling, made of brick, with curls of smoke rising from its chimney.

'A man will be well hidden in a place such as this,' Arent said. 'A place for woodsmen and trappers, if I'm not mistaken – people whose natural inclination is to be separated from humankind.'

Ann turned, looked him square in the eyes.

'Because we are poor and seek solace in nature does not mean we are without pride, sir.'

'I did not intend to sound as if I were ungracious, dear lady ...'

Ann cut in. 'Wait here,' she said as they neared. 'My sister's temperament is delicate and she must be forewarned.'

The rain had eased now; the grey, thunderous clouds had given way to a clear blue sky. Arent looked out across the rolling grasslands, at the mystery and darkness of the forest, at the line of the stream cutting into the landscape. He found as he was waiting that if he walked a few paces towards the edge of the incline, skirting the water, and craned his neck, he could see the harbour mouth and the expanse of sea beyond. Was that a stout sailing ship, he wondered, drifting elegantly towards the channel where the *Adventurer* had sat at anchor in the hours before their ill-fated mission? Arent now realised it was the frigate taking his crew to France. He gave a sigh and a wry smile, safe in the knowledge that Cadwaller would see them all safely home.

Ann appeared, beckoning him towards the front door. He sidestepped a chicken that had fled the coop, grabbed its neck and gathered it into his arms. Bethsany stood nearby, wiping her hands on her apron. Arent passed the bird over and introduced himself. She nodded, opened the shack's small wooden door and roughly pushed the bird in.

The dwelling was warm. A pot of soup bubbled on the brazier. Arent looked at the two women with curiosity – sisters, different in both looks and temperament, living away from the town among outliers, tinkers and those too ill at ease to make themselves known to the world.

'Please, be seated,' said Ann, indicating a chair at the table. Arent watched as the women went about their work – Bethsany stirring the pot, Ann organising bowls, spoons and a half loaf of heavy dark bread for their meal.

After Ann had said grace they began to eat. As he picked up his spoon, Arent decided he must try hard to concentrate on his manners. But he needn't have worried. While Ann sat straight in her chair taking nimble portions of the broth onto her spoon, Bethsany lifted her bowl to her mouth and drank it down in the same way a lusty sailor would drink a pitcher of ale.

'You have sailed from Rotterdam, Mr Arent?' said Ann. Arent answered that yes, that was indeed the case, and asked her how she knew such a thing.

'The market place is a fount of knowledge,' she said. 'Even the smallest boat's whereabouts are well tracked by eager eyes and commented upon. A ship the size of yours, involved in a gun battle, will always be the subject of much curiosity by locals.'

Bethsany took another generous slurp of broth from her bowl.

'We are merchant sailors, that is all,' said Arent. 'The intelligence we were given was incorrect. We were told Fairfax was still some days away from the town.'

Bethsany drained her bowl and rose abruptly from the table.

'Do not be alarmed, Mr Arent,' said Ann. 'There are jam patties to follow. My sister does not want to see them burn.'

Arent nodded, ran a piece of bread around his empty bowl in order to soak up the last of the broth. He noticed Ann's eyes flicker in his direction and wondered about the strange sisters' existence high above the town.

'Are you native to these parts?' he said.

Ann smiled. 'Yes. My sister and I have lived here all our lives. The sea, the sands, the great hills, our church – they are all that we know. And what of your country?'

Bethsany set a plate of jam patties onto the table.

'Ours is an industrious nation,' said Arent, scrutinising the small jam delicacies. 'However, the landscape is much easier to navigate. It is mostly flat, mistress, like the deck of a ship.'

Arent began to eat. The patties interested him. They were shaped like an almond and half crimped around the edge.

'Most times they're filled with meat and vegetables,' said Ann. 'And sometimes a single end will be made sweet with jam.'

'So, a man might carry one around in his pocket,' said Arent, 'and have a choice of two meals — one savoury, one sweet?'

Ann laughed at this. When he had finished his third helping, Arent complimented Bethsany's skill, telling her that he had eaten in many different parts of the world and in his opinion her patties could not be bettered. Bethsany wrapped two patties in a square of cloth and presented them to Arent, that he might have use for them at breakfast.

After Ann had helped Bethsany clear the table, Arent readied himself to retire for the night at the dwelling of Elowen's grandmother. He thanked the sisters for their compassion towards him. It had been a rare day, he said, a statement that Ann readily agreed with.

14.

(i)

Even though Elowen had managed barely three hours sleep since handing over to the day patrol, Kettleby was forced to wake her. The garrison had been ordered to form up on the parade ground. Soldiers went about seeking out the occupants of each dwelling, women and children included. Richard Arundell took up his position in front of the turret, standing rod straight as he waited for the castle's inhabitants to assemble. Then a sergeant major yelled for quiet. When the only sound to be heard was the lapping of the ocean waves, a figure emerged from the north building's entrance. It was the governor, Sir John Arundell.

A short, elderly man with wisps of white hair circling a bald crown, he was dressed in full Royalist uniform. His ceremonial sword boasted a bejewelled hilt. His jacket was embroidered with the Arundell family crest. Uncertain on his feet, he stood next to his son. The sergeant major called the garrison to attention. For many it was the first time they had seen the governor in the flesh.

Elowen, in her role of honorary sergeant, stood with other officers a pace behind the aged governor. Kettleby, as ensign, stood alongside her, holding the royal standard. A child began crying and an officer shouted for silence else quiet would be imposed by his sword. His harsh words echoed across the parade ground, sending fear into the women's hearts.

Sir John Arundell was passed a rolled parchment. He held it up for the garrison to see.

'The traitor Fairfax has offered terms of surrender,' he said in a strained voice. 'I have refused. The garrison at Pendennis will never bend to those who seek to usurp the power of our king. We will stand our ground. We will defend the castle until we are victorious. And if God determines that we must give up our lives to do so, then that is what we will do.'

He began to cough then, a hoary cough that seemed to echo beyond the castle walls and rise across the ocean. Richard Arundell moved to help his father but was irritably waved away. The old man turned and shuffled back from whence he came.

There was worse to come. As women and children assembled outside the storeroom, it was announced the daily ration allowance had been reduced by half. It was not unexpected but still brought a gasp of horror. The failure of the Dutch frigate to land its cargo had led to many conflicting rumours. Some said more help was on its way; others said that it had merely been a forward vessel, sent in preparation for a full invasion. It was well known that the Prince of Wales and his mother, Queen Henrietta Maria, had fled abroad to organise a mercenary army. They would not give up on proud Cornishmen and women who stood for the king. Others, of a less optimistic nature, were not so sure. The governor was a drunkard, they whispered, who was willing to let the garrison starve while he filled himself with rare, salted beef. What's more, there was no mercenary army ready to cross the sea and fight Fairfax because the king had already been defeated.

(ii)

At night, as she patrolled the battlements, Elowen considered the circumstances under which she had discovered Maben. She kept her distance now from the other troops.

'Sergeant Elijah, why has Fairfax not attacked?' they asked her, mockingly. She did not supply an answer. They laughed from their lofty lookout posts, looked at her with contempt, pointed at the slingshot tied around her waist. A strange one, they said – a boy who looked like a girl. A sergeant in name only, who had somehow found favour with a prince.

During her night patrols, Elowen began to spend time with Maben in the stables. She had deposited him there after they fled from the raggedy-girl and the devil-man with red eyes, knowing that the animals would help calm his sensitive nature. There were twenty horses in all, including the three that had been tethered to the Prince of Wales's carriage. There was little hay left for them to eat and a lack of food and exercise was beginning to show in their physical appearance and uneasy temperament. They were easily agitated, snarling whenever Elowen entered, as if her inability to offer them sustenance was an act of well-measured malice.

She invariably found Maben asleep in the hay corner. His sudden addition to the castle population had not been commented on. And Elowen could always point to the boy's ability to calm animals, so as to justify his presence. The three black horses especially responded to Maben's care, allowing him to stroke and nuzzle them as if they were long lost friends.

'Are you awake?' she asked. He smiled, his eyes moving rapidly in their sockets, his mouth caked with grime, his hands leaden with dirt. She watched as he went through the stables with a pail, offering water to each animal. If only she were able to find a regular source of food. She had considered sending him back to Ann and Bethsany but was frightened of the temptation he would face if he passed by the girl and the devil man in the forest. The castle, she considered, was the best place for him although the thought of Ann's distress at his disappearance played on her mind.

In the days following his rescue, Maben had shown Elowen the key. At first she was angry and scolded him for re-visiting the corpse of the royal footman. Then, as quickly as it had flared, her anger subsided as she reflected on the contents of the chest, the trinkets that lay therein. The old gods were at work, she was certain. It was they who had guided the boy to the footman's pocket. She took Maben in her arms, felt guilt wash through her. The boy, in his short life, had been scolded enough.

Elowen returned to the makeshift shelter she shared with Thomas Kettleby and crawled inside. He was sleeping soundly. He had left her a mug of ale, a piece of bread and something that looked like dried fish. She drank the beer and left the rest, made herself comfortable on the hessian matting and tried to sleep. As she did so, she heard Kettleby stir and turn himself towards her.

'Elijah?' he said in a sleepy drawl. Elowen felt him draw close, his breath suddenly warm on her neck. 'Elijah, I'm cold,' he said, 'colder than I've ever been. When will it end,

Elijah? When will it end?'

In an act of comfort, his arm reached over her shoulder. She lifted it and pushed it away. He chuckled in his sleep, allowing his arm to reach over her once again. Elowen took hold of his hand with the intention of pushing it back once more. But his hand was ice cold, so she held on to it while she slept.

15.

(i)

Dan Arent said goodnight to Ann and Bethsany and walked the half mile to the dwelling where Elowen had lived with her grandmother. The flimsy door was secured with twine. Arent cut it with a fish knife given to him by Ann and entered. The inside was as cold and musty as the *Adventurer's* stinking hold. It was dark, too. Ann had also given him a candle and some kindling wood, as well as an extra blanket. Arent took a tinder purse from his knapsack and sparked a ball of dry brittle moss. He transferred the flaming ball to the hearth and added thin strips of wood shavings. Soon a healthy fire was burning. For the first time in months, Arent felt able to relax.

He took in the meagre contents of the place – hearth, bed, table, chair. He speculated that the old woman had slept in the bed and the girl had slept upon a pile of matting that lay in the corner. He was surprised the old woman had lived for so long. It was a grim existence here in the wilds beside the forest – a simple place for the crazed and the disturbed of mind. And now, Arent ruefully thought, I too have washed up here. He felt a sudden coldness – his wife's hand, perhaps – brush against his brow.

As the dwelling warmed, he again took up his knapsack,

emptying it of its remaining contents: bowl, twine, sexton. Hidden at the very bottom was the letter addressed to the governor of Pendennis Castle.

Arent considered it for a while, then ran the gutting knife along the seam of the waxed, folded parchment. The letter he took out was brief and to the point. It read:

To the governor of Pendennis Castle, the most honourable and loyal Sir John Arundell.

It is with pleasure that I send you kegs of powder, match, beef and other such provisions in order that your garrison might prolong the defence of Cornwall from Parliament's army. And yet my pleasure has been disrupted by news that His Highness the Prince of Wales was unable to bring a consignment of plate, silver and other such jewels which I reasoned upon to be used for further relief in the form of an army of men. Until such time as this consignment is received, or other funds requisitioned, I can confirm that I am unable to send assistance. This, of course, pains me greatly. My only hope is that you may continue to repel the traitor Fairfax from the loyal south westerly part of our blessed isle without further aid from England's loyal subjects in exile. God save the king!

His majesty's servant,

Sir Paul Pindar.

Arent knew that the Prince of Wales had fled overseas. And now he learned that he had been unable to take with him a box of treasure to spend on mercenaries. He re-read the letter and folded it back in its original shape. So, this was Pindar's great plan for which he was willing to pay so handsomely, and which had now been dashed – to entrust the *Adventurer* in the landing of a small army. Arent settled himself on the old woman's bed. Governor Arundell would be disappointed; surely the only course left to him was surrender? And by delivering the letter to the castle, Arent was certain the garrison's surrender would be immediate. After all, why prolong such suffering when all hope of further supplies had disappeared?

He had just lit his pipe when he heard a snarling animal outside. He took up his knife and prepared to defend himself. The animal's snout was tight against the base of the door. At once Arent thought of the forest and of the wild dogs that might live there, preying at night on vulnerable souls as they slept.

'Gallant! Gallant! Heel, I say!'

It was Ann Netherton who was calling. Arent moved to the door, opened it, revealing Ann who was holding the hound by the scruff of its neck.

'Mr Arent, my thoughts have been churning and so I decided to take in the night air. I forgot that on occasion the animal will come and sleep by the door in anticipation of his mistress's return.'

Arent smiled. 'I have not yet taken to my bed. Come in before you freeze. I have made the place warm.'

Ann entered, leaving Gallant to roam outside. Arent dusted the seat of a chair in readiness for his unexpected guest.

'I must apologise to you, Captain ...'

'No, good lady – an apology is not needed ...' he said.

'Oh, but there is. My conduct as I stood before Arwenack House was reprehensible. Emotion overcame me. I hope you understand.'

Arent nodded. 'I understand, madam. You have endured

the loss of a child. You are, therefore, within rights to feel aggrieved.'

'Poor Maben is an innocent,' said Ann, 'without capacity to fully understand danger and shield himself from harm's way. I pray for him and hope that he has come together with dear Elowen in that foul place.'

They fell into a period of silence as Arent tried to make sense of it all. What made her so sure the boy had gone to the castle, he asked.

'I know him,' she said. 'He will go in search of his good friend. The question I am unable to answer is, why? What has spurred him onwards towards her? Why does he not find our love sufficient?'

Arent jabbed at the fire. He knew nothing of the boy and his intentions. Nor did he understand why the girl Elowen had fled to Pendennis. And yet the depth of Ann Netherton's sorrow moved him to a point where he yearned to help resolve the issue.

'Is there a way into the place?' he asked.

The question startled her. 'Why, no. How can there be? It is a fortress. It is under siege.'

'Yet I've heard it said there are deserters – soldiers who have fled.'

'Many have fled,' she said. 'And can anyone blame them for their escape? Some are no more than boys, dressed up and handed a musket they struggle sufficiently to carry. The distress mankind heaps upon itself is without end.'

He re-fired his pipe with a stick from the hearth. 'So, if

there are deserters it stands to reason that there is a way out; and therefore, a way in, wouldn't you say?'

Ann considered this. 'Yes, but … why would anyone want to attempt such a thing?'

Arent smiled. 'I stayed in this town, Mistress Ann, precisely to gain access to the fortress. I have a great need to speak with the governor. A letter is to be delivered on behalf of certain supporters of your king. But first I need information, to find a way inside. Do you know where I might find it?'

Ann considered this. 'The ale house, Mr Arent. All manner of folk congregate there — cut-throats, deserters. It is a godless place, filled with men sinking into their cups.'

Arent smiled. 'You speak with a bitter edge, Mistress. Are those souls any less deserving of God's mercy?'

Ann hesitated. Was he trying to make a fool of her? 'All are deserving, Mr Arent, if only they would open their hearts to the Lord.'

'And what of a man who once opened his arms and praised God's mercy, only to see his loved ones tossed away like flotsam in the sea?'

'Such a man is being tested, I would say. Faith has to be earned, Mr Arent. The harder it is achieved, the greater its reward.'

She gathered her cape around her neck. Arent tapped the edge of his pipe bowl against the hearth. He stole a glimpse of her then, her face illuminated by the flames, the knot in her hair slowly loosening as she shifted the garment into position around her, like a flower, struggling to unfold itself.

She looked up at him; he averted his gaze.

'What is the nature of this letter, Captain? Are you at liberty to tell?'

Arent hesitated. 'It concerns certain plans to help relieve the castle.'

'That can only be a good thing, although I fear I detect doubt in your voice.'

'The plan involved the delivery of funds to raise an army overseas. The army would have been transported to this place on my ship. According to the letter in my possession, that army will not now materialise.'

Outside, Gallant began to whimper as if struck suddenly by the sadness of Elowen's absence.

'I have heard, Mr Arent, from the gossips in the market-place, that the Prince of Wales's carriage came to an unseemly halt as it travelled the road into our town.'

Arent, intrigued, said, 'This I have not heard, Madam. To what end?'

'It remains something of a mystery. One of the prince's footmen cannot be accounted for. The gossiping tongues are certain that his disappearance is the result of foul play.'

The captain tapped his pipe again, harder this time. 'Surely the prince would have informed the governor?'

'I cannot say. The truth is locked behind the castle's walls. The governor is old and fierce in his service to the king. Whether the new commander – Fortescue – has been handed information on the mystery, I do not know. Perhaps the good Lord is working his will and the governor is ripe to be compelled to surrender.'

Arent began to think over a number of possibilities. If it were true that the footman had somehow stolen treasure destined for Pindar in Rotterdam, the governor of the castle was resisting surrender under a false pretence.

Gallant began scraping the door. Ann Netherton stood, brushed her skirt, ready to leave. 'I must sleep, Mr Arent. Then we will talk again.'

Arent bowed. 'I have enjoyed your company, Madam. And I thank you again for your help and hospitality.'

Ann, revealing her shyness, gave the briefest of smiles. 'Goodnight, Mr Arent. May the Lord be with you.'

He stood outside and watched as Ann and Gallant made their way in the darkness along the trackway. Whatever the true circumstances of the incident with the prince's carriage, one thing was clear: the stubborn governor of the castle needed to be told that relief would not, after all, be forthcoming.

(ii)

Before he slept, Arent stoked the hearth with fresh logs. It was well past midnight. At first, he could not sleep – there were too many things playing on his mind. Only when the atmosphere in the tiny dwelling grew warmer did he drift into a dry, heavy half-sleep. The dreams that had plagued him these past three years returned. They were like old friends, reappearing suddenly after short periods of absence, as though they were stored somewhere deep in his mind, ready to appear at a moment's notice. His wife always seemed close by – a physical presence, in need of his support – and as his dreams advanced into realms that had hitherto remained resistant, Arent shed himself of the blanket given to him by Ann.

He found himself on a quayside, awaiting the day's catch. The sea was dark, the sky overcast. It seemed that he was the only one waiting. There were no boats, no other shapes or forms on the quay. 'There is nothing to eat, husband, and the children are hungry,' said Arent's wife, a distant voice, addressing him from unknown corners of this moody dreamscape. Where was she, he wondered? He could not see her. The dream faded as quickly as it had arrived.

He did not wake, as he usually did, with cold sweats and in a disturbed temper. The dream had been replaced by images of a new house and an unknown foreshore. Arent twisted and turned on the old woman's bed. It seemed colder now; the fresh logs had burned down; the night winds had begun to penetrate the nooks and crannies of the flimsy dwelling. Arent pulled Ann's blanket over himself and caught her scent. He slept soundly.

16.

(i)

The day following Sir John Arundell's refusal to accept Fairfax's terms of surrender, Elowen was woken by the sound of an explosion. A few moments passed, then she heard the most terrible screams. At first, she wondered if there had been a collision in the harbour. But the screaming was of such intensity that Elowen knew it was much nearer. She crawled out of the shelter to stand witness to what had gone on.

It was seven o'clock in the morning, that time of day when the families of the soldiers cleared up after breakfast. Children were usually playing, the women sweeping or else making adjustments to their shelters. The day patrols had already taken up their positions on the battlements. Elowen, feeling groggy, watched as soldiers ran across the parade square. It was a difficult situation for her to comprehend, especially after a long night walking around the castle grounds.

'What is it?' she asked a woman. 'What's happened?'

'Ordnance,' she was told. 'God rest those poor innocents – God rest the souls of those poor babes.'

A missile had been fired by a cannon placed along the Parliamentary army's forward positions, somewhere on the hill that led to the headland. A direct hit had been made on one of the temporary shelters near the castle's eastern wall, killing a mother and two of her children. Elowen walked cautiously towards the scene, even though the prospect of confirming such terror with her own eyes scared her.

For some reason she stopped; she became aware that the birds had given up their singing. A strange sense of compression forced the air around her as a second missile whistled overhead, coursing its way into the castle grounds. She watched as it followed its murderous trajectory, sucking life out of the atmosphere. But the gauge proved incorrect. The missile landed on empty ground near the southern most wall, leaving a deep, gaping depression in the earth.

'Elijah – stay where you are, I beg you. Do not venture forth. It is too painful to see.'

Thomas Kettleby stood before her, eyes etched with fear.

'They are firing at us?' she said as if she were in a dream. 'I saw the second missile drop from the sky ...'

And then another came, the rush of air even louder than before. People were running across the parade ground in all directions now, screaming in terror. A loud thud indicated that the missile had again overshot the parade ground, landing near the stables.

'Maben!'

Elowen ran; Thomas Kettleby, angry and confused that she had ignored his warning, followed her. As Elowen reached the lower level of the castle's grounds, she saw that the missile had hit a small brick house to the side of the stables, a depository for timber, saddle bags and rope. It had blasted a gaping hole in the wall, rendering the building unsafe. The stables, though, were intact. Elowen ran inside.

'Maben? Where are you?'

The horses were distressed – rearing, turning, pulling on their tethers, flanks heaving.

'Who are you searching for?' said Kettleby. 'Who is in here?' And Elowen suddenly realised that the ensign knew nothing about Maben's presence, in the same way that he knew nothing about the murder of the footman and the other deceptions she had instigated.

'Maben!'

She expected him to be curled into a ball, hands over his ears, screaming. Instead, she found him comforting a grey mare. She embraced the boy and followed Maben's lead, helping to calm the most distressed of the animals. Kettleby, puzzled by the wispy boy and his role among the horses, felt obliged to do the same. He filled a pail with water from the trough and offered the beasts water. As he did so, he looked at the boy named Maben with a curious mixture of interest and jealousy.

(ii)

The shelling stopped. For the rest of the day, the garrison went about its business with a chill weariness. The dead were wrapped in heavy blankets, buried in open ground near the south wall, and the blood that remained on the parade ground was covered with earth. The traumatised children were offered extra rations despite the strict ruling imposed by the governor. As dusk fell, weariness turned to anger and shots rang out from the battlements as soldiers fired indiscriminately at a number of small vessels zig-zagging in the harbour. Who was sailing in these vessels wasn't clear and the shot fell well short. But it didn't seem to matter. It felt as if a minor blow had been struck against Fortescue and Fairfax in honour of the dead.

Elowen found it difficult to sleep. She lay on her bed shivering, the thought playing on her mind that, for any one of the thousand or so people trapped within the castle, annihilation was a mere moment away. In the afternoon Kettleby brought her food. They sat together in their shelter, sharing ale, dried beef and bread. He asked her about the boy in the stables, whether Maben was her brother. Elowen shook her head. She told him that Maben was a neighbour, that he helped her trap animals in the forest. Kettleby remained silent, trying to stem a feeling of aggrievement at the existence of this unexpected friend: this thin, ungainly boy who was unable to speak the king's English.

Outside, a rumour was heard that Fairfax had offered more generous terms of surrender. With food becoming scarce, it was surely only a matter of hours before the old governor accepted the inevitable and led the garrison out with muskets held high. But a counter-rumour started, indicating that stubborn John Arundell had waved Fortescue's messenger away, telling him that every man, woman and child in the garrison had pledged to die rather than surrender. It was also said that Arundell was waiting for a great army from Europe to arrive – an army that would liberate England and set the king once again on his throne.

Still shivering, Elowen fell into extreme tiredness. Kettleby wrapped her in his own blanket and told Richard Arundell that honorary sergeant Elijah was sick with fever. The *de facto* deputy governor gave Kettleby a disinterested look and ordered him to take over Elowen's night-time duties. Kettleby tried to summon the courage to ask for an increase in rations, but Richard Arundell's angry demeanour dampened any thought of doing so. Used to a regular sleeping pattern, Kettleby struggled to keep awake during the night. On more than one occasion, soldiers discovered him slumped against a battlement wall, asleep. These men took great pleasure in humiliating their weak superior, on one occasion holding a lighted torch directly above his head, causing him to wake and scream out in anguish while they laughed with contempt.

At dawn, Kettleby crawled into the shelter and lay close to Elowen. He wrapped his arms around her, buried his mouth in the nape of her neck. As he re-ordered his blanket, he became aware of a pungent fluid smeared on Elowen's legs. He shook her until she woke, stared in horror with fearful eyes.

'Elijah!' he said. 'God's mercy be upon us! You have been shot!'

17.

(i)

Dan Arent and Ann Netherton entered the grimy waterfront tavern. Clusters of men sat before rough-hewn wooden tables; others stood against the damp brick walls, deep in ribald conversation. In the darker recesses — small alcoves situated at the farthest end — women and boys entertained sailors with whispers, laughter and more.

Ann covered her mouth to offset the stench of the place. 'This is a truly foul establishment, Mr Arent,' she said. 'God did not intend for us to become promiscuous and dissolute.'

Arent nodded in agreement. And yet the sweet aroma of tobacco hanging in the atmosphere brought equally sweet memories of nights spent in the taverns of Rotterdam. Surely, he thought, God was able to distinguish between dissolution and merriment? It was the devil who led folk astray, who tempted men to wander beyond their rightful boundaries.

'Show me the proprietor, Mistress,' he said. 'The sooner we glean our information, the sooner we may leave.'

She pointed to a bearded, grey-haired man wearing a leather apron and holding a large jug of ale. Arent approached as the man set the jug on a table before a group of sailors.

'My question is short,' he said to the proprietor, 'and I have coin to procure a speedy answer. It's been said that you are the man who can tell me what I need to know.'

The proprietor wiped his mouth with his sleeve. He looked at Arent with suspicion. 'You are a fugitive,' he said, 'an' the lady is a well-known bible thumper who I've seen many-a-time preachin' in the square. The answer to your question will cost you dear.'

Arent held out a purse – a purse given to him by Ann – in an attempt to soften the man's prickly nature with the jangle of coin. The proprietor reached to take it. Arent snatched it away.

'A group of soldiers escaped from the castle for two days since. Tell me, where do they hide?'

The proprietor snarled. 'What's it to you? Why d'you seek 'em? To betray broken men to that devil Arundell?'

Arent shook his head. 'Information, nothing more, nothing less. A boy is in great danger. Those men can help me save him. Take me to them and the purse is yours.'

The proprietor took on his heavy cloak and led his visitors out of the tavern and down a stinking alleyway further along the street. The tide was low, the water lapping gently over the harsh black harbour rock. Along a raised promenade, accessed by cobbled steps, stood a number of dilapidated sheds – fisher huts and store-shacks, well-placed for hiding contraband. Arent smiled as he guided Ann, gently holding her arm as she negotiated the slippery surface. At high tide it would be difficult to access the ramshackle buildings. Even though the Roundheads had taken control of the town, Royalist sympathisers were always ready to punish those who worked against the king. The sheds were perfect for deserters who might need to make a quick getaway.

The proprietor knocked on one of the doors.

'Open, friends. I have brought you fish, bread and ale.' A moment of silence elapsed before Arent heard the sound of movement inside. The door opened but an inch and the proprietor asked to be allowed inside. But when Arent came into view, suspicion was raised. Panic set in and an attempt was made to shut the door. The proprietor swiftly leaned in, his ample form preventing the door from closing.

'Haste, my friends, is an ill virtue. I've brought a man whose presence here will be to your advantage,' he said.

Arent now caught a glimpse of the face that was determined to lock them out. It was the face of a boy, fifteen or sixteen years old – the face of a soul living in constant fear.

'I am not here to do harm; I am in need of information,' said Arent. 'This lady who accompanies me is a servant of the Lord. Her son has been lured to the castle. His liberation is all we seek.'

There was further to-ing and fro-ing with the door. Then, pacified by Arent's words, the boy stepped back, allowing unfettered entry. Inside, the musty shed was a tangle of nets, pots and other fishing equipment. The boy and his friend slept like harbour rats, each in a corner on a pile of dirty sacks. Ann was minded to cover her mouth and nose once again, the fish and seaweed being most distasteful.

'What will you?' said the boy who had opened the door. He was thin and gaunt, with dark eyes slowly sinking into their sockets.

'I wish to enter the castle,' said Arent.

The boy laughed. 'Can't 'e walk o'er the moat bridge an' knock the gate?'

Arent's face hardened. 'I'm not for games, boy. You are a deserter, liable to be punished. If you wish to remain at liberty, then you will tell me how I might enter in a more secretive manner.'

The boy, taken aback by Arent's rising anger, settled into seriousness. 'Then the postern gate be best,' he said. 'The guards there an' all can be bribed, if 'e wishes to leave – though I's not heard of a man offering good money to go in.'

Ann stepped forward, holding her cloak tight around her. 'I believe there is a boy in the castle – my son. He has entered, seeking his friend, Elijah. Do you know of him?'

The boy looked over to his companion who was sitting on the matting, knees pulled up to his chin. Then he said to Ann, 'There's many thar's inside, Mistress – near a thousand, so's they reckon. And rations 'ave been cut. There's children, ay, wit empty stomachs churning wit fear. There's one named Elijah I know of: 'e saved the king's son and heir. Ran an assassin' through with a flagpole so they say. And he's as sharp as a pike when it comes t' handling a slingshot. They say 'e can hit a tree's bud at a hundred paces.'

Ann whispered, almost to herself, 'Elowen!' to which the boy shook his head and said: 'No, Mistress – Elijah is 'is name.'

Arent had heard enough. 'Does the guard have a name?'

'They'se all got a price, Mister. Jus' tell 'em Abraham Biggs sent 'e. And say I's warm and boasts a full belly since the day

I got me out of Mad John Arundell's wretched hell.'

(ii)

The hill road beyond Arwenack House was alive with canon and Fortescue's troops, so Ann led Arent to another steep trackway which lay behind the small grey stone church.

'This will take us to the sea front road without the likelihood of being arrested,' said Ann. 'From there we can scale the path from the foreshore to the southern-most castle gate.'

Arent, eying the imposing climb before him, muttered that he'd rather take his chances with the New Model Army. Ann graciously ignored him.

He found himself once again trying desperately to keep up with her. This time he was determined not to rest or disrupt her burning desire to reach the boy. He knew that even though her faith conferred upon her a redoubtable calmness in times of anguish, a lingering sense of unease existed, in the same way that doubt had existed in his own mind. As he climbed, Arent touched Pindar's letter. It sat snug in his pocket, the feel of it reminding him that a crumpled patch of parchment offered the best chance of putting an end to the siege, not only for Ann Netherton's boy, but for all those who found themselves imprisoned within the castle's high walls.

Once they reached the crest of the hill, the ground flattened and Arent found himself, at last, on the straight – a narrow path that wound through scrub, grassland, and an ancient burial ground. There were few dwellings in these parts; the ones they passed were no more than primitive bothies, the kind that existed in Arthur's day. Arent contemplated asking Ann if they could shelter for a few minutes, even though it would mean breaking his silent promise to persevere until they reached the castle. As if she were reading his mind, she turned and said, 'We are close to the sea front, Mr Arent. There is a place nearby where we can rest ourselves.'

Sure enough, a brief rise in the land led them to an expansive view of sea, sand and rocky shore, and in the distance the great headland, framed by a billowing dark sky, on top of which sat Pendennis Castle.

Arent collapsed on the damp grass, stretching out his tired legs. Ann remained standing, gazing at the fortress, secure in the knowledge that Elowen and Maben were there.

'This war,' said Arent, removing one of his boots, 'is proving hard on the feet.'

'And yet you willingly came to it,' said Ann.

Arent, kneading the sole of his foot, said, 'Ay. And I'll willingly be leaving it behind once I deliver Pindar's letter and you have your boy safe in your arms.'

'Yet, the war will grind on, Mr Arent, regardless of what interventions we are able to make. The weal turns; suffering endures.'

Arent was kneading his other foot now, and yet the sullen tone of Ann Netherton's words stung him in the same manner as the blisters on his feet. She had a solemn, far-away look in her eye that he found disconcerting.

'Mistress Ann, I lost my faith after a great tragedy befell me. I have found your faith a source of strength in our short dealings together. Do not lose it, Mistress. Do not make the same mistake as I.'

She looked at him then and smiled. 'Faith or no faith, you are a good man, Mr Arent.'

A moment passed between them during which an easterly wind rattled the trees and rustled the grass all around before sweeping across the land. Ann pulled her cloak tight. 'Come now, Mr Arent. Set your boots tight on your feet and let us make our way before darkness and rain begin to fall.'

'Yes,' Arent said, struggling with his laces. 'Let us venture forth with renewed vigour ...' but she had already strode a good number of paces along the trackway, leaving him talking to himself.

18.

(i)

Hell was a parade ground where hundreds of men, women and children lived.

Hell was a barrack room where soldiers lay burning with fever.

Hell was the time spent waiting for when Fortescue ordered the canons to fire.

Hell was the ordnance that tore innocent souls asunder.

Hell was the gnawing gash of hunger that every member of the garrison felt as their lives seeped away.

Hell was Pendennis Castle.

*

Old man Arundell stood at the window in the governor's room. It was an overcast morning. Mothers and their children went about their daily business as best they could – attending the cooking fires, administering to the infirm, repairing their flimsy shelters. Soldiers patrolled the battlements and the castle's perimeter walls, keeping a fair eye on any unidentified ships at sea or suspicious figures that lurked among the trees. The governor had received from Fortescue a third request to surrender. He looked upon the parchment in his hand as if it was a personal insult of the highest order.

'Sir, I have the latest figures regarding the dead and wounded.'

It was Arundell's son, Richard, speaking. He was standing in the middle of the governor's quarters, anxiously awaiting his father's attention. Sir Abraham Shipman and Major General Molesworth stood behind him. Sir John remained at the window.

'Sir?'

Old Sir John was in no mood to listen to his son prattle on about the dead. What was done was done. It was God's will. Blame Fairfax and the Roundheads if blame was to be apportioned. He turned irritably and went to his seat, throwing the parchment he was holding onto his desk.

'I will not accept their terms of surrender,' he said. 'It is an outrage what they demand without authority from the king. To give up this place would render upon me the indelible character of treason. I would rather bury myself, and all of those wretches outside, before I deliver it up. Nothing they can threaten is as formidable to me as the loss of my loyalty to the king and my own conscience.'

He sat, hands clenched, absorbing the silence that followed.

Sir Abraham Shipman was the first to summon courage and offer a reply. 'Our food stock is rapidly waning, sire. The children who you once saw darting pillar to post now lie in their shelters with the vacant mark of hunger upon them.'

Sir John brought down his fist. 'Then make good the situation, sir! Take yourself to the stables. Inside there is meat enough, I grant you.'

Richard Arundell shifted uneasily. 'Sire. The king's horses reside in our stables. Surely you are not suggesting ...'

'Yes! Yes, I *am* suggesting, sir. They reside within my jurisdiction. They are instruments granted to me as weapons in this war. Now go, I say; put an end to them – whether they belong to the king or no – and leave me be!'

(ii)

Richard Arundell left his father's quarters. He walked down the steps from the first-floor apartments and onto the parade ground. The order to kill the garrison's horses had left him feeling uncomfortable. He had an affection for the animals but knew that in a time of crisis sentiment must be placed to one side. He called over a senior officer and told him to gather seven troopers who were at ease firing a musket at close range and not afraid of carrying out bloody work. As Richard Arundell went on his way a new, nagging thought regarding the three black horses from the king's stables crossed his mind. What if the king saw fit to punish him? As the officer in charge, and despite his father's bombast, he might find himself accused of high treason. He considered returning to the governor's quarters and asking his father to clarify the point. But he desisted. Sir John would be well into his cups now, a time when his anger knew no bounds.

After crossing the parade ground, Richard Arundell saw a small crowd gathered on one of the battlements beyond the stables. The crowd was leaning in amongst the crenels, looking down towards the sea. He heard cheering, as well as shouts of great merriment. He walked towards the battlement, curious to hear the nature of the crowd's interest.

A man shouted down. 'A boat, sir! A boat has made a sally and broken through!'

Arundell ran up the stone stairs and pushed his way to the front. A shallop with a single sailor on board had managed to negotiate its way through Batten's blockade. The tide was low, and the small boat was dragging at anchor. Richard Arundell saw three of the castle's soldiers clambering over the rocks, ready to gain purchase of much-needed supplies.

'It's a blessing from God, sir. A blessing from the Lord.'

Arundell watched as the men struggled with what looked like sacks of grain. The crowd moved along the battlement in the direction of the southern-most gate, eager to see the abundance of what the sailor had brought them. It took a while for the soldiers to climb the steep path; but when they arrived they were greeted with a rousing welcome.

The welcome, though, soon dissipated. Inside the sacks were three hogsheads, swedes, turnips, and a flagon of ale. The cheering was transformed into dismay. Sensing anger, Richard Arundell ordered the crowd back onto the parade ground. As they went, he saw seven musketeers marching roundly towards him. Yes, he decided; he would shoot all of the horses – even the king's – and let his father deal with the aftermath.

(iii)

Maben was sleeping in the corner of the stables, in the musty area where hay had once been piled. Now there was not even a single brittle stem, only empty hessian sacks in which the hay had been delivered. Occasionally the horses looked towards the corner and whinnied in fear, as if they knew that death would soon be their master.

The boy woke suddenly and rubbed his eyes. She was standing over him – the raggedy girl who, as yet unbeknownst to him, was his twin sister. He sat up, pushing himself away from her. She was wearing the same clothes – old boots, a long dirty skirt and a thick knitted jerkin that smelled of lime. She crouched beside him and whispered in his ear: 'They are coming.'

The girl walked over to the window and beckoned him towards her. Seven of the garrison's soldiers as well as the deputy governor were making their way. Maben saw muskets, bandoliers, swords, sharp cleavers.

'How are you going to save them?' the girl whispered again.

There was no lock on the stable door for him to turn; no implement for him to repel the soldiers. The horses reflected his nausea; they began pulling sharply on their ropes, eager to show the full weight of their distress. Maben started to tremble. The raggedy girl laughed. He covered his ears and began to scream.

As he did so, the door opened; Richard Arundell entered. He ordered his men to stand in a line and prepare their muskets, all the while staring at Maben and the girl.

'Quiet, I say!' he shouted at the boy. 'In damnation, I say, quiet!'

He struck Maben with his crop; the boy fell to the ground, panting, yearning. Then Arundell took hold of the girl by her hair and dragged her towards the hay corner, close to Maben's bed, where he threw her down. She looked at him with disdain and hissed. Arundell moved towards her, ready to strike again. But he stopped; there was something strange about her eyes. The girl hissed again and this time he saw clearly what had stopped him from encroaching further: her eyes were turning red, as if blood had seeped from her brain into her sockets. Arundell shivered at the sight before saying: 'What in the name of the Lord are you?'

A shout went up; his men had filled their pans and were ready to take aim. Arundell was about to call over a soldier and give the order to put an end to the girl; she had a contagious affliction, he surmised, a vile, unknown disease that might sweep through the castle like a plague. The horses began to buck, whine, rear their front legs, even though they were constrained by ropes around their necks. Now Maben crawled between them, slipping each rope from its hook, setting the horses free. The beasts shook themselves out, twisting to face the soldiers before the first match could be lit. The girl hissed again – a sharp, primordial sound that electrified the air, charging each animal with a defiant spirit.

Arundell, too, was becoming anxious, unsure as to where this mayhem would lead. He gave the order: 'Fire!' But the commotion of the horses – their anger in the face of their would-be killers – proved too much. The beasts began to flail with their front hooves and buck with their hind legs, forcing the soldiers against the stable's wooden panels, and thus preventing a true aim that would lead to a kill.

'Fire, I say! Fire, damn you!' shouted Arundell and it was now that a wayward shot blasted into the roof, antagonising the beasts more. The girl began to laugh now – a sharp, high-pitched laugh that seemed to signal it was time to leave. Cowering and pleading beneath hooves, screaming beneath the staggering weight of the horses, Arundell's soldiers could contain them no longer, the bucking anger of the animals tramping them to the floor. The stable door opened, and the first horse bolted through, followed by the rest. They galloped wildly across the flat ground over where the victims of the first bombardment of the castle were buried and towards the open south gate. Richard Arundell cursed his men and ordered them to give chase. He ran outside, shouting, 'Close the gate, I say! Close the southern gate!' A shot was rendered, bringing down one of the stragglers, a grey. The rest of the horses disappeared amongst the trees beyond the castle's boundary wall, the same trees that had harboured the Prince of Wales's would-be assassin. The fallen animal was swiftly dispatched. Arundell, his anger having escaped from the bounds of rational thought, went back into the stables, his crop high and ready, feverish with contempt. He entered and his eyes scoured the empty space before him: the witch-girl and the mute boy had disappeared.

19.

(i)

Dan Arent and Ann Netherton climbed the rising track that led to the castle's southern-most gate. It was late afternoon and a blustery north wind was sweeping across the sea. Ahead of them the woodland poplars and elms, buffeted by strong winds, drooped and swayed on the steep headland.

'Wait!' said Arent as the gradient became more challenging. 'Let me rest for a moment.'

Ann stood as the Dutchman sat himself on a log, catching his breath. For the first time she began to doubt whether he was up to the task of helping Maben escape. God was testing them, sending them to a place of hardship and terror. Arent, she reminded herself, had surrendered his faith; he was liable to fall at the first hurdle.

'Once we reach the gate it would be beneficial if you stay hidden, Mistress,' he said, rising to his feet in a slow, heavy manner. 'Allow me to negotiate our entry with the castle guards.'

As he spoke, Ann was alerted to movement among the trees. 'Look,' she said.

Two horses – a grey and a powerful black – were wandering along a lower trackway, digging their hooves into the soil as they steadied themselves against a fall.

'Do you think they are from Pendennis?' asked Ann.

Arent, suddenly roused, said, 'Let us hurry along, Mistress. The sight of loose horses makes me fearful.'

After a few more minutes of the climb, they came to the smouldering remnants of a fire. A large boulder, smooth and indented, as if it had been fashioned into a seat, was set facing the glowing embers and the sea beyond. It looked to Arent like a throne of sorts, and he tried to imagine the person who had occupied it. Seeing Ann's concern, he said: 'Vagabonds, no doubt, hiding from Fortescue's troops. Come, let us continue.'

But Ann resisted. 'There is a story that concerns these parts,' she said, 'a story about the devil and how he was made angry by the building of the castle. Do you know of it?'

Arent confessed that he did not, so she told him – about how the devil would sit at the summit of the headland until King Henry's castle banished him from his vantage point. 'They say the devil sits here still, under cover of darkness,' she said.

'And you think this piece of old rock is evidence?' said Arent in a jaunty tone, trying to make light of her uneasiness.

She didn't answer. Instead, she walked close to the boulder, gently laid her hand against the smooth stone, before pulling it away, the warmth of it unnerving her. They walked on.

As they neared the summit, Ann, who was a few paces ahead of Arent, saw that the castle gate was open. She told him but once again he was struggling, unable to conquer the final stretch of track.

'I am in need of water, Mistress,' he said. 'My lungs are fit to burst, and I fear my throat is stricken. I must sit awhile before we enter.'

'Wait then. I will continue,' said Ann. 'There will surely be water beyond the castle's high walls.'

Arent watched as she strode purposefully along the track, between the last of the trees, and disappeared. He sat panting, embarrassed at the toll the gradient had taken on him. He closed his eyes, swept the palm of his hand across his brow. Then something – a rustle of leaves, or a sudden gust of wind – made him look up. Staring at him from a distance was a girl, aged no more than ten or eleven summers – a raggedy-looking girl whose bloodshot eyes made Arent gasp in terror.

(ii)

Thomas Kettleby sat beside Elowen with a cloth and a bowl of dark water. He dipped the cloth in the bowl once more, wrung it out. Tentatively he began to wipe her legs until the last of the dry blood was gone.

'I thought you'd been shot,' he said. 'I thought a terrible thing had happened. But I've seen this infirmity before. My sister had the same – a visit from the Moon Queen she called it.'

Elowen stared at him. She felt embarrassed as well as proud. Ann Netherton had told her about bleeding, said that God had made woman in a strange and complicated way. When the bleeding did not come, Elowen thought herself inferior. Her grandmother never touched on the subject; she was so old Elowen thought she had forgotten.

'Now you must attend to yourself,' said Kettleby. 'I have done what I can. I should not gaze upon you any longer.'

He crawled out from the shelter. Elowen took the cloth from the cloudy water and squeezed it as hard as she could. She pulled at her heavy undergarments and began wiping between her legs. The blood had stopped now. Her dizziness had abated.

*

She must have fallen asleep because she heard 'Elijah, Elijah – can I come in?' as if in a dream. She sat up, realising it was Kettleby. She said yes, and then, as he crawled into the shelter, she felt tiredness wash over her once again, and lay down her head.

Kettleby laid an assortment of cloths and dock leaves before her. 'My sister said a woman must prepare for when the blood comes again. You must keep yourself clean otherwise you will not be welcome in the world.'

Elowen took up a piece of cloth and a leaf. Kettleby told her to place the one on top of the other. She did so and Kettleby turned his head as she slipped it between her legs. When she was done, he told her to rest.

'I will go in search of food. I have entertained the children awhile and been promised an end of bread.' He began to stroke her cheek. 'Poor Sergeant Elijah,' he said. Elowen held his hand as she felt the onset of sleep and light-headedness engulf her once again.

(iii)

As she walked through the southern gate, Ann Netherton was

confronted by a group of women and children. Their faces were brushed with fear and anger. Many of the younger children, who were being either dragged or carried, were crying.

'Get away from here!' one of the women said to Ann. 'Get away!' As the group hurried through the gate, they shouted: 'Free at last! Praise God, we are free from this hell!'

Beyond the stables, Ann saw another group making its way, and behind them others – including men in uniform.

'Quickly – the gate is open!' someone shouted. Ann at once felt anxious and foolish. Who on earth would walk into this place when everyone else wished to escape? Only the thought that Maben was somewhere within the castle grounds prevented her from turning and leaving with the rest.

She made towards the parade square. The deprivation shocked her. She saw women and children wandering aimlessly to and fro, their vacant eyes and pallid faces telling the story of the siege. A young girl poked the remnants of a smouldering fire; a man sat exhausted with his head in his hands. At the opposite end of the parade ground an argument ensued between troops tasked with distributing the meagre rations and beggars desperate for any extra scraps that might come their way. Everywhere was chaos. And all the while those strong enough gathered what they could and hurried towards the open southern gate.

Ann stopped. She watched as a young man emerged from a makeshift shelter, carrying a dishful of water. He threw the water over the low wall that edged the parade ground and began to wring out a filthy cloth. '

I'm looking for a boy who goes by the name of Maben,'

Ann said to him. The young man shook his head. 'There's no boy who goes by that name, Mistress, not that I've heard of.'

He crawled into the shelter. Ann turned towards the great turret and the single-storey building which, she suspected, housed the commanding officers. No sooner had she taken her first steps, than a weak voice carried towards her: 'Mistress Ann! Mistress Ann!'

The voice came from the shelter from where the young man carrying the dish of water had appeared.

'Elowen? Praise God! Is that you?

'Yes, Mistress. Yes …!'

Ann closed her eyes and whispered a prayer, thanking the Lord for guiding her safely through such terror.

(iv)

Once inside the shelter's stinking interior, Ann took Elowen in her arms. She was disturbed by how weak the girl was. What had happened to make Elowen, who spent hours stalking prey in the forest, such a pale shadow of her former self?

'She has bled,' said Kettleby, as if he had anticipated Ann's silent question.

'Where, dear Lord? A wound?'

Kettleby shook his head. 'In her private parts, Mistress. I have knowledge of such things. I have a sister who …'

'We must remove her. Make yourself ready. We will each carry her. Elowen – are you able to walk?'

Elowen, in her drowsiness, nodded.

173

'Then let us get to it. The gate is open; dear Elowen, be strong! Once we reach the south entrance, a friendly face will meet us – a Dutchman, a sailor named Arent – who will help take care of you.'

'Will you stay with me, Mistress?' said Elowen, her voice faint, brittle.

Ann said she could not. 'Tell me – do you know where Maben is?'

Elowen's head rolled to her shoulder as consciousness deserted her for a moment.

'Elowen! Elowen!' said Ann, shaking her. Elowen's eyes opened as she burst into life. 'Where is Maben?'

Elowen's mouth was so dry she could barely speak. Her cracked lips struggled to form the shape of her words.

'The stables,' she whispered, to which Ann Netherton nodded. 'Then we must go there now and save him.'

Ann and Kettleby each took up the girl's weight and hauled her out of the shelter. Then, having implored Elowen to use all her might to stand, they began to walk – slow, careful steps, bearing her as best they could, following the weak rhythms of her sickness. Kettleby let it be known that Elowen was wrong; the boy Ann was seeking was not in the stables after all. He had disappeared.

'There were happenings,' he said. 'Strange things that never in all my days have I seen. The governor wanted to shoot the horses, but the horses reared up and bolted, as if they had come together as a unit of fighting men, eager for battle.'

'Mistress,' Elowen whispered. 'If there was violence in the stables ... it must have disturbed Maben. And there is a girl I have seen ... a strange girl ... whose demeanour mirrors that of Maben's.'

Ann considered this. Elowen was rambling, she knew, and so she turned to Kettleby.

'Where should I search? Did he escape through the gate? Is he hiding amongst the trees?'

'The girl is with him,' said Elowen, her strength failing, Ann and Kettleby heaving her upright once more. 'I have seen too many horrid things during my time here, Mistress, many a horrid thing.'

As they approached the stables, a shout went up. They stopped and turned. Richard Arundell, accompanied by a troop of soldiers, was marching towards the postern gate.

'Away! Away!' he said. 'Do not cross the threshold or by God you will pay for it!'

The appearance of the governor's son caused a great deal of apprehension for those who were preparing to flee. He ordered the soldiers to secure the gate. Panic ensued as desperate souls pushed and shoved in their determination to exit the castle grounds. The soldiers fell upon them, striking those who resisted with the butts of their muskets, threatening anyone who refused their orders with the lash and worse. Kettleby, Elowen and Ann remained where they were as the dreadful scene played out. Ann looked on in despair. When the last lucky few had slipped out of Pendennis Castle, the soldiers pushed shut the old wooden gate.

It seemed to Ann that their only chance of escape had

been lost. Those left behind were dispersed by the soldiers, branded as traitors and dissemblers. Future punishment, they said, would be swift and harsh. Ann feared she would never find Maben. Worse: if ever she returned without the boy to the dwelling high above the town, Bethsany's grief would be all consuming.

Richard Arundell was near to the southern wall now, his anger rising at the number who had fled. He shouted at two guards standing on the battlements.

'Open fire!' he ordered. And, to the soldiers who had accompanied him: 'Man the battlements! Put those deserters to death!'

The two soldiers Arundell had barked at seemed to hesitate in carrying out the order. Instead of making ready to fire beyond the castle wall, they pointed their muskets towards the soldiers readying themselves to climb the steps to the battlements.

'Stay where you be!' one shouted. 'If you value your lives, do not take a step further.'

Ann recognised one of the men: Dan Arent.

Richard Arundell urged his soldiers on, despite the muskets aimed in their direction, urged them to scale the steps and show courage before the imposters. But Arundell's soldiers remained where they stood. Arent and the other man swept their muskets right to left, with a threat that any false movement would result in bloodshed. Arundell repeated his order to scale or else face court-marshal. The second man now shouted, telling Arundell to desist. But the governor's son repeated his order for a third time. The second man lit a match, guiding it towards the musket pan.

Before he could ignite the powder a whistling noise punctured the air, followed by a heavy dull thud of metal ripping through wood which in turn gave way to an explosion. Large splinters showered the open ground, onto the soldiers, women and children who stood within the vicinity. Fairfax's army had begun another bombardment. The stables had taken a direct hit.

20.

(i)

Ann found herself on the ground, such was the power of the missile's impact. Drifting smoke, the smell of sulphur, a strange throbbing in her ears that turned into a fateful echo in her mind; yet still her thoughts returned to Maben.

She stood, uncertainly; her disorientation induced odd feelings of passing through an invisible gate, of circling her remonstrating body, of a merry sickness deep inside that seemed to lie on the cusp between life and death. Screaming and shouting perforated the air. She looked towards the bodies lying all about. Elowen had escaped the worst; Kettleby, struggling to rise, was looking at her, his anguished face mouthing words that she could not hear.

Arundell, too, was wounded; splinters had pierced his eyes. He was being attended to by one of his men – one of the "spineless maggots", so he'd called them, who had refused to storm the battlements. She knew all this because she passed by them, erect now, her arm tightly gripped by Kettleby and another man. Her ears were still ringing but not as much as before. God had shown His mercy. They were walking towards the gate.

'A short distance is all that is required,' Kettleby said. 'Elowen follows us – directly behind, walking of her own volition.'

Ann could hear what Kettleby was saying but was unable to turn her head, so she focused on what she could see before her: the gate, the castle grounds strewn with the wounded, the frightened and the lost. The bible spoke of Hell as a place of fire and damnation. Ann had preached the requisite sermon in the market place many times: 'A place of molten lava, the walls coursing red, the naked bodies of sinners speared for all eternity by disciples of Beelzebub.' But Hell, she now thought, was not so. It was a place of acrid smells and broken beauty, where good men festered until their brains could take no more. And Beelzebub's disciples were not pot-bellied dragons with pointed tails but men like Arundell who quietly went about their own form of destructive, intimidating business.

'Mistress Ann! Mistress Ann! Praise God; praise the lord that you are alive …!'

It was Arent who, on the other side, was the one holding her, his ample frame wrapped around her like a bear protecting one of its cubs. For that brief moment she gave herself to him, allowed herself to be taken in by his presence. All thoughts of God, Hell and the Devil drifted from her mind. She was shivering and shaking, but she could feel the warmth of him, and for that brief moment it soothed her.

'Hurry, friends. Make your way to the gate.'

Another man was speaking, the man who had stood with Arent on the battlement. Ann, Elowen and Kettleby were pushed towards the wide-open entrance as yet another of

Parliament's missiles whistled above them. Its trajectory, though, was flawed. It crashed into the castle's eastern wall sending an explosion of brick and stone into the air but avoiding human flesh. Once through the gate, Arent guided Ann and the others along a descending trackway leading to the sea. It proved too steep, too demanding. Ann collapsed onto the ground; Arent stood over her and lifted her beneath her shoulders until she was settled against a tree.

'I must find Maben,' she said.

'Please, Mistress Ann,' said Arent. 'This is not the time. See there, at the water's edge? Small boats lie in wait to ferry us into the town. Who knows how many more missiles will rain down this day.'

Ann struggled to get up. 'I must find him, I must …'

She grabbed hold of a willing hand that offered to pull her to her feet. The man whose hand it was looked familiar – the second soldier on the battlement, who, along with Arent, had pointed a musket at Arundell's men.

Seeing the uncertainty in Ann Netherton's face, the man introduced himself. 'The name's Cadwaller Jones, Mistress – deputy captain of the *Adventurer*. Pleased to make your acquaintance.'

Ann, in her anguished state, pulled her hand away from Cadwaller Jones who she immediately took to be all too forward in his dealings. She looked around for Arent but he'd disappeared.

'Mistress Ann,' Cadwaller Jones said. 'There's one here amongst us who knows where Maben is.'

Ann, though, was having none of it. Arent appeared again but there was nothing he could do or say to convince Ann Netherton that Cadwaller was telling the truth. However, the imperative to find the boy was too strong; Ann's desire to protect Maben was overwhelmingly resolute.

'Arundell's soldiers will soon appear with orders to fire upon those who have fled the castle's grounds,' he said.

'Let them fire ...' Ann murmured, her mouth and throat dry, her fingers stiff and brittle with fear. Elowen held out her hand and Ann took hold of it.

'Now,' Arent said to Elowen, 'tell us once and for all: where can we find this strange boy named Maben?'

(ii)

Daylight was beginning to fade. Through the trees, the sea had taken on a mournful, iron-grey colour. The sky was restless – billowing dark clouds.

Shots were heard from the battlements. Arundell, his one eye still bleeding, had ordered his troops to open fire on the small boats rescuing those who had managed to escape from the castle. The south gate had been locked, a semblance of order re-imposed. Within the castle grounds, men, women and children lay wounded and dying on the grassy square where the shattered stables stood. Arundell did not care that the shots fired at the small boats were to little effect. It sent a message to those below in the harbour: Pendennis Castle would not surrender.

Outside the southern gate, the narrow trackways that zig-zagged the steep decline to the water's edge caused problems for Arent and the group. Horses stood uncertainly in their path, unsure of which way to go. Elowen, her strength gaining with each step, gently coaxed one of the king's beasts towards her, whispered in its ear, softly stroking its throat latch. The horses they came across answered with harsh grunts or with frightened bucking movements. Elowen watched a nervous mare that suddenly bolted downhill, resulting in a terrifying scream and fall. Sometimes it was difficult to distinguish the various sounds: did a particular scream belong to a stricken horse? Or to one of the many women and children hiding amongst trees, scared out of their wits that Arundell was about to seek them out with his bloodthirsty soldiers? Saddest of all were the constant laments of the wounded, pleading for water, comfort and mercy as they lay hoping for salvation, their souls already beginning to slip away.

Arent's group followed an undulating line. Elowen, leading, was the first to see flames – bright, dancing flames cultivated, she knew, by the raggedy girl and the strange red-eyed man who was her master. She edged forward until she could see the figures more clearly. The scene was as before: the man sitting before the fire on the great smooth stone that Arent had christened the Devil's throne, the girl standing opposite; and, near the fire, she saw a heartless, soulless Maben dancing a tired jig.

Elowen beckoned Arent, pointed for him to see. 'There!' she said. Arent looked on, took in the disturbing nature of the scene.

'Stay here,' he said to the others. 'Cadwaller will accompany me. We will bring the boy to you.'

They edged in the direction of the fire. Darkness was creeping ever closer; the cries from the castle were distant but could still be heard.

'What plan is in your mind, Captain?' said Cadwaller. His face was stern, uncompromising – like it was when they had argued on the deck of the *Adventurer*.

'I'll take the boy,' said Arent. Then, pointing towards the dark figure, 'You remain close to that wretch over there.'

Cadwaller was pleased with this. The girl, with her dry fair hair, her long filthy skirt, and her witchy face, scared him more. The man seemed settled where he sat, although Cadwaller was only able to see the back of him: black coat, buckle shoes, a wide Puritan hat.

Arent felt that the three figures were each endowed with their own peculiar menace. Why was the boy dancing? he wondered. It was as if he was carrying out some form of penance, undergoing punishment for an unknown sin. The dark figure occasionally twisted himself from right to left, left to right, his broad back moving in a single graceful wave.

Arent moved level with the fire, opposite the dark figure, and said in a clear, commanding voice: 'Maben! Put an end to your merry ways and come with me, boy. Hurry! Mistress Ann awaits you.'

The fire continued to crackle; Maben continued to dance. The raggedy girl stared into the fire; the dark figure remained seated, his face unseen behind the lop-sided brim of his hat.

Arent stepped towards the fire – commanding, definite movements. He took hold of Maben's arm and forcibly dragged him away. The girl said something in an unfamiliar language – gritting her teeth, clenching her fists, a shibboleth of harsh, unruly words. Arent pushed Maben into Ann Netherton's arms. The boy looked up at her in a sullen daze.

'This way,' said Cadwaller. He began to move along the trackway, pointing towards a winding descent that would lead them to the sea front. From there they needed to continue over the rising land in order to avoid Parliamentary positions before they were rewarded with a clear route into town. Arent and Cadwaller knew they had to evade capture. They were escaped convicts. If they were intercepted, then Fortescue, they were certain, would not be so accommodating to their cause.

The dark figure began to turn. As he did so, Elowen felt the air change, as if an angry current of breath was disturbing the atmosphere. Slowly the figure stood, his face still obscured. But he began to draw back his head far enough to reveal what Elowen feared: reptilian eyes … eyes that seemed inhumanly narrow in the fading light, like those of a snake or a dragon, the colour of them adjusting to the dusk, losing their reddish brightness, turning burgundy, indigo, a deep unsavoury purple. The figure let out a fearsome scream that carried through the thin trees, over the castle walls and beyond. A gush of foul air followed – putrid, deathly, as if hewn from a secret chamber deep within the earth.

'A beast is upon us!' said Cadwaller. 'A beast of burden, sent to do the Devil's work.'

Maben struggled in Ann's arms, recoiling from the sight and stench of the creature.

'Stop, Maben! Stop, I say!' but she could hold him no longer. The boy slipped her grasp and ran back to his position by the fire where he immediately began to reprise his awkward, disjointed jig.

The dark figure laughed now, although the sound, at first sharp and clear and penetrating, soon heaved and bubbled as if a whirlpool was trapped in the creature's chest. Arent strode forward once more. To Maben he said, 'I command you, boy. Leave here now and follow us to your rightful place.'

No sooner had the words left his mouth than Arent was swept onto the ground. There was no reason to it – it was as if the earth or gravity had been pulled from beneath his feet. A clue lay in the demeanour of the dark figure: his hands – thin, wrinkled, blotched with warts – were now extended in the direction of the stricken Arent. An invisible force had been delivered, so powerful it had rendered the Dutch captain helpless, at the mercy of his foe.

Cadwaller went to his aid. He, too, became a victim of the dark figure's wrath. Another burst of laughter pierced the evening air, followed by gurgles and wheezing unlike anything heard from within a human form.

The fire seemed to re-ignite, the flames soaring to new heights even though no extra wood had been set upon it. Arent and Cadwaller remained immobile, satisfied, it seemed, to lie on the ground, staring at the oncoming night sky. The girl watched over them; Maben continued to dance. The dark figure wiped his mouth with his sleeve, seating himself on the great smooth stone, his shoulders slowly twisting as before.

Time, it seemed, had stopped.

Only Elowen was able to sense the true nature of the beast lurking beneath the long black coat and Puritan hat. Her grandmother had recounted to her the tale of the castle's building, how King Henry's men had been too scared to venture forth onto the peninsula, fearful of what might be waiting there. A legend existed that the tip of rock was the Devil's domain and that he sat overseeing the great expanse of ocean, guiding ships into the shallows and rejoicing in the sight of sailors buffeted against rocks. The wind had drawn the Devil away – strong gusts took his hat, sending it flying towards the trees, the same trees from which an assassin had sprung, intent on doing to death the Prince of Wales. While the Devil chased his hat, King Henry's men had moved in and built the great castle. Ever since, the Devil had remained on the hill, eager to do his worst.

Elowen untied her slingshot, set a weighty stone from her pocket into its leather cradle. As if suddenly aware of the danger, the Devil unravelled himself until he was once again standing, his piercing eyes trained on his foe. Kettleby stepped backwards, distraught at the sight of the hideous figure before him, as Elowen began to swing the weapon round and round above her head – faster and faster than she had ever done before. Ann Netherton crouched along the wayside as the slingshot unleashed its single piece of ammunition, whistling as it tore up the air.

Elowen's aim was true. The stone registered a direct hit. It struck with such force that it lifted the dark figure off the ground, knocking him backwards. He came to rest in a bramble bush and lay there, senseless but not dead. Not only had the stone struck the head of the wretch, but it had dislodged his hat, whereupon the wind carried it with great velocity into the air and towards the lapping waves within the darkness beyond.

'Elowen, you have knocked the cur to silence,' said Kettleby. 'He does not move, he does not threaten.'

The raggedy girl looked on in disbelief, anger in her eyes, before melting into the trees.

'Magic!' whispered Elowen.

'Or perhaps a trick of the night?' said Kettleby. Elowen nodded; she could not be entirely certain of anything that had happened these past days.

(iii)

They hurried along the sea front in order to evade Fortescue's soldiers. Arent led, Cadwaller following close behind. Kettleby supported Elowen; Ann kept a firm grip on Maben's arm. It took many hours in the darkness to negotiate the track, thick with mud, a sharp northerly wind biting at their necks. Occasionally they would stop and look back at the castle's battlement fires blazing above a cold restless sea.

It was past midnight when they arrived at Ann Netherton's dwelling. Bethsany, still awake, took Maben in her arms. She said she would scold him for his disappearance in the morning. Elowen begged her forgiveness – Maben had merely wished to seek her out. Bethsany said she held no grudge and took Elowen into her arms as well.

After each had found nourishment with the broth that simmered over the fire, Arent lit a torch and led Cadwaller and Kettleby to the empty dwelling further upstream. Gallant appeared from the forest. The old dog bounded towards

Arent, growling and barking, eager to protect Ann, Bethsany, Elowen and Maben from harm. But he quietened when he caught Arent's scent, allowing the Dutchman to pat and pet him until his old heart was content.

'We'll light the brazier and let the hound keep us safe while we sleep,' said Arent. Cadwaller grimaced at the very sight of the beast and once Arent was soundly asleep, he mused, he would push the dog outside.

Cadwaller, though, was the first to fall to slumber followed soon after by Kettleby. Arent lay awake, his mind alive with all that had passed. The letter to the castle's governor was still in his pocket. What use was it now, he wondered? Why should he try to sway the mind of a stubborn man of eighty years, deep in his cups? And yet Arent was pained as he considered those poor souls who were left, enduring Arundell's merry hell and the wrath brought down upon them.

He got up. A sense of great disillusionment had suddenly befallen him. He opened the door and stepped into the darkness, taking in the cold night air. Gallant stirred and Arent allowed the dog to join him outside. The night sky was clear, the stars and moon bright. He had been wrong to try and enter the castle. Why hadn't he considered another way of delivering the letter to the governor? Surely, once the old fool was aware that no funds would be forthcoming, he would give up his irrational attempt to hold the castle for the king? A new strategy was needed; perhaps handing the letter to a stranger was the answer, a stranger who would deliver Pindar's words, for a price, to Fortescue. And yet Arent was still not convinced such a plan would work. Did Fairfax wish to make an example of the garrison? Did he wish to inflict the harshest punishment on those who languished within?

Arent's thoughts dissolved in an instant. Across the grasslands, illuminated by the moon's silvery light, he thought he saw a figure prowling near the stream. Arent strode in its direction, Gallant at his heels.

(iv)

It was the hound who first recognised Ann. Gallant ran to her, licked her hand, then turned his attention to the stream, disappearing down the rain-soaked bank.

'You too are unable to sleep, Mr Arent?'

He stood before her. 'I confess there are a number of things weighing on my mind.'

Ann pulled her cloak tight around her. 'It is becoming a habit for the two of us. My thoughts are filled with the horrors of the castle. And I have been thanking God that Elowen and Maben are safe and with us once again. I thank you and your associate, too, Mr Arent.'

Arent bowed his head. 'Cadwaller is a good friend. We have sailed together for many years. He was due to return to Rotterdam with the other members of my crew. I thought he had done so but he disobeyed my order, surprising me with his presence after you entered the southern gate.'

'I will thank him later when calm has returned.'

Gallant leapt to the top of the bank and shook out his fur. They watched him pick up a scent, turn this way and that with his nose to the ground. Gradually he drifted in the direction of the forest as if enticed by some invisible wonder.

'What are your plans, Mr Arent? You are still a convict — likewise Mr Cadwaller. Do you intend to stay here, in hiding?'

Arent pulled out the letter from his trouser pocket. 'No, lady. I have decided to deliver Pindar's letter to Colonel Fortescue. I can only hope that he shows himself to be an honourable man.'

Ann shifted uncertainly. 'I will come with you,' she said, 'and plead to the commander. The slaughter must be stopped.'

'No, Mistress. It is too dangerous. There is the possibility that I may be arrested. It is a gamble that only I can undertake.'

'And your friend, Mr Cadwaller?'

'I will leave it to you to explain to him my actions. If I am unsuccessful and imprisoned, then tell him he must return to our country. I can see no other way.'

'You are a good man, Mr Arent. I will pray for your success. You will always be welcome here, whatever the outcome.'

Arent took a step towards her, took hold of her hand. As he did so, the door of the dwelling opened. Elowen appeared.

'Forgive me. I heard your voices and the plan to petition Fortescue. But there is something you must see, Mr Arent … something which may help you reach the successful conclusion you seek.'

(v)

It was dawn when Elowen, Ann and Arent breached the threshold of the forest. They followed the track that led to where the Prince of Wales's carriage wheel had snapped, bringing it to a screeching halt. Before they reached the forest's end, beyond which the footman lay beneath a pile of leaves and branches, Elowen made a diversion. She led them to an aged oak and began to pace out a number of steps. 'Here,' she said and told Arent to begin digging with the small shovel Ann had brought with her.

It didn't take very long for Arent to uncover the wooden chest. The soft moist soil gave way easily, the chest lying barely a few inches from the surface. Arent lifted it without great effort, brushed the wood so that the Prince of Wales's crest could clearly be seen. The three stood in silence for a while, looking down at this most royal object. Elowen reached into her pocket for the key.

'Wait with that,' said Arent. 'Not here. Let us carry it and set it down indoors upon a table. That way we can examine it at our leisure.'

And so, Elowen and Arent shared the burden of the chest, each gripping a side handle, while Ann walked behind, uncertain of this new mischief that had been brought upon them.

When they entered the dwelling, Bethsany and Maben were up, preparing for market day. Kettleby and Cadwaller were sitting next to the brazier. They watched as the chest was set down, its fine wood and brass casing catching their attention.

'What have we here, Captain?' said Cadwaller.

Arent remained silent and took hold of the key. As he was about to spring open the lock clasp, Maben kissed the tips of his fingers and laid them on the lid of the chest. He looked at Elowen in a moment of silent affirmation. They would say nothing about how the chest had made its way into the forest, nor would they speak of the other incident. The footman would continue to lie in peace; nobody would know.

The riches they saw contained within the chest were beyond their wildest dreams. Gold, silver, diamonds, amethyst – all in the form of rings, bracelets, gorgets, and necklaces. There were coins, too: gold sovereigns, tightly packed amongst the treasure. And there were curios: tiny ornate figures; diamond studded thimbles; miniatures of Charles the king and his French queen, Henrietta, who had fled overseas from the castle in the same manner as her son.

Ann crossed herself. 'Lord in his heaven! What is this?' she said in a breathless, unbelieving tone.

'Treasure, I'd call it,' said Cadwaller. 'Treasure that was marked to finance human cargo for the *Adventurer* and bring more poor souls to slaughter.'

All except Bethsany had a hand in the chest – even Maben was gently caressing the shining bracelets, lockets and brooches or else twisting items encrusted with gems in order that refracted light might fully highlight the magical colours therein.

'It is a trove the likes of which we'll never see again,' said Kettleby.

'But what of its destination, Mr Arent?' said Ann. 'It belongs to the king. These are objects sacred to the throne.'

Arent sighed before answering her with a sharp, impatient edge. 'Do you expect the slaughter to end if it is returned to your king, good lady? I very much doubt it. These trinkets will be sold to, the highest bidder, the money invested in muskets and men. No, I will not return it to your king. I will offer it instead to Colonel Fortescue.'

Cadwaller dangled a ruby necklace before his eyes. 'To what end, Captain?'

'In order to retrieve what is rightfully ours, Cadwaller. I have a letter and a chest to bargain with – two items that might enable us to retrieve our ship and leave this godforsaken place once and for all.'

21.

(i)

Before he left, Arent made Cadwaller promise that he would not interfere.

'Keep the chest safe and locked,' he said. 'And – this is important – hide the key in a place only you know.'

Cadwaller agreed. The two men embraced. Arent said farewell to Elowen, Kettleby, Bethsany and Maben. Then he turned to Ann, took hold of her hand and kissed it.

'There,' he said, 'at last, I have done it.' She blushed slightly and wished him well. Arent smiled. 'Colonel Fortescue is an honourable man, I am sure of it,' he said. Then he made his way along the track, across the open grassland until he descended the hill and disappeared.

Arent kept the brim of his hat low as he made his way towards the town square. Traders were beginning to ready their wares for market – fish, vegetables, hand-sewn cloths, pheasants tethered by their feet. He passed by the wharf from where he saw the *Adventurer's* mast standing true between several other ships taken by Fairfax's army. A group of soldiers idled nearby. Arent bowed his head and hurried along.

He walked through the town's main street, past the beer

hall where he and Ann had spoken with the two deserters, past the little stone church, round the bend which led to marsh and open ground until he was able to see the turrets of Arwenack Manor, one of which remained blackened by the fire that had raged when the Royalist forces had retreated. Soldiers were stationed outside the entrance. The steep road leading to the castle where the murderous canons were fixed was still blockaded by ordinance and carts. Arent took a deep breath. He pushed out his chest, took the letter from his pocket, and advanced towards the guards, who immediately stiffened and ordered him to halt.

'My name is Arent,' he said. 'Captain of the *Adventurer*. I have a letter that I wish to hand to Colonel Fortescue.'

The soldiers hesitated. Arent certainly looked familiar. Where had they seen him before?

One of the men shouted towards the doorway, his words echoing along the manor house's long hall. Another soldier appeared – a man with a faint air of authority. He looked the Dutchman up and down. Arent held up the letter and repeated what he'd already said.

If the new man – a sergeant by all accounts – had listened in good faith, he wasn't about to show it. He ordered the guards to take the Dutchman into custody. 'This man is a criminal,' he said with a jab of his finger. 'A danger to the public good.'

A struggle took place during which Arent waved the letter and called Fortescue's name several times. It was to no avail; he was unceremoniously marched back along the high street and frowned upon once more by the cold merciless God of his own bad luck.

(ii)

When Bethsany and Maben arrived in the market square, Dan Arent had already been deposited in the town jail. They didn't see him – how could they? – even though the Dutch captain was only a few yards away from them, below ground in the same cobbled cell in which he'd languished once before.

Bethsany and Maben had a routine on market day which they always adhered to: Maben would lay a rough hessian blanket on the ground, then Bethsany would take from her basket her wares and pass them, one by one, to the boy. Today there were barley cakes and eggs, and socks and mittens that she had quietly knitted during the evenings as she sat beside the brazier. She passed Maben a thick long-stemmed punnet of rhubarb which had been tied with string and carried like a quiver of arrows on her back as well as several bottles of Elijah's cider. The boy neatly set out each item, leaving a corner of the blanket clear for him to squat on as they waited for prospective customers. Bethsany sat on a wooden box, brought to her as usual by one of the market labourers whom she paid with a barley cake.

They sat until mid-day. The eggs, rhubarb, cakes and cider sold quickly and, with the proceeds, Bethsany sent Maben to buy bread, fresh milk, mutton and a bag of apples for Elijah's brewing. The money left over would be placed in a leather pouch and hidden under Bethsany's bed.

As the crowd thinned, she told Maben to roll up the blanket. Then the two of them began the walk home. Half-way up the hill, Bethsany turned once again into a lane. The boy knew where they were going. He began to drag his legs in order to indicate his displeasure. Bethsany stopped, showed Maben the back of her hand. With a sullen look, the boy turned and followed her.

They reached the old woman's cottage. She was sitting, as before, in the same dimly lit room. She smiled when the boy appeared; Maben, indifferent, averted his eyes.

Bethsany eased herself into a chair. She took an apple and a barley cake from her basket, handing them to the old woman. Bethsany said – slowly, almost to herself – that today's market had been busier than the last to which the old woman nodded as if a great nugget of wisdom had been imparted.

Maben squatted on the floor. He wished they'd gone straight home. He'd rather be following Elowen into the forest, checking the animal traps. He supposed that she was with her new friend, the one they called Kettleby. Maben watched as the old woman struggled to her feet and stoked the fire. As she did so, he recalled dancing on the headland, the flames flickering beneath the night sky. And he suddenly remembered the strange figure with red piercing eyes who seemed to whistle a haunting tune even though his lips remained sealed.

"Maben!"

The boy looked up. Bethsany nodded towards the door. Standing there was the girl. He didn't recognise her at first; he squinted before finally realising who she was. He recalled how she had visited him in the castle stables and they had sat together with the strange figure on the headland. Now she looked different. Her hair was no longer matted; nor were her clothes filthy and torn. Instead, she wore a pretty blue skirt that reached beyond her knees and a clean white shift tied with a belt. Her dry hair had been parted, styled with two pigtails held in place with strips of blue ribbon. She wasn't angry, with dark haunting eyes, as she had been before. The girl offered Maben her hand and smiled; she wanted to lead him into the garden.

'Be off with you,' said Bethsany, 'and be easy in your play-making.'

The grass was still long. Maben felt the soft fur of stems and flowers against his arms as the girl guided him along a narrow pathway. Her hand was larger than his, the skin smooth and firm. He noticed she was wearing thick socks beneath her ankle boots. He studied her feet – small and graceful in the way she stepped over branches that had fallen onto the path, the hem of her skirt brushing against her legs as she took purposeful strides, negotiating her way.

'Sit here,' she said, settling before a tree, drawing her knees to her chin. She watched him as he placed himself before her, aware that he was frightened, uncertain as to her intentions. Maben remembered the last time they had been together in the garden, the way she held the large black beetle; he shuddered as he remembered the rest – the insect held over her mouth, the cruelty of what she did. He looked at her hands, gripping her knees. The callouses along her knuckles had disappeared.

She brought out a small parcel from a pocket within her skirt – a cloth held together with string. She lay it on the ground, untied it, revealing a mixture of boiled fish, dry meat and bread.

'Eat,' she said.

Maben did so. The girl stared at him, smiling. Was she really his sister? He wasn't certain. She must be somebody close to him, like Bethsany, Ann, and Elowen; why else would he be brought here? He squeezed a lump of fish between his fingers. Perhaps the old woman was Bethsany's sister? Sometimes it was hard for Maben to understand exactly who was who. The man with the red eyes, for example; Maben wondered if he was his father.

The girl snatched the cloth, even though there was still some meat left to be eaten. 'A game,' she said. 'I want to play a game. First you must close your eyes for me. And promise not to look – do you promise?'

Maben nodded. He could feel a sudden shift in the air as she stood, heard the rustling of her skirt. He kept his eyes shut even though he longed to open them and observe her moving around him. He shuddered as she tied her neck scarf around his head, adjusting the material so that his eyes were fully covered.

'I will tie it tightly, boy,' she giggled, 'because I know if I leave it loose you will peek after me.'

He sat in darkness waiting for something to happen.

'Count to one hundred,' she said. 'Then you may come and find me.' Maben moved his head, first this way, then the other. Her voice seemed distant – he could hear her laughing, along with birdsong and sea water and the rustling of leaves. Maben was not able to count to a hundred. He could barely count to ten. And so, he remained in darkness, rubbing his legs, catching the scent of her from her scarf, uncertain when he should remove it and go in search of her. He didn't want to go searching before time – she would be angry, and he certainly didn't want her to be angry with him. But the darkness was beginning to feel uncomfortable, as if he was buried beneath a pile of leaves. He began to grow restless, agitated, like the time he knelt and cupped his ears as the Prince of Wales's carriage thundered along the road.

He could wait no longer. Maben stood, pulled the scarf from his eyes. He began to walk about the garden, searching for the girl. Was she hiding in the long grass? He saw a pile of long branches stacked against a wall – soft, rotten branches covered with flecks of mould and green mildew. He thought of the footman, of the man's bulk, and how he was felled by a single stone against his forehead. The girl wasn't hiding amongst the branches. She was nowhere to be seen. Had she played a trick on him? Had she turned back into a raggedy girl?

'Maben!'

It was Bethsany, shouting from the side of the cottage. But Maben wasn't ready to go home and wouldn't be until he found the girl.

Bethsany called him again – a sharper tone this time – and Maben knew he had to acquiesce. She was already walking towards the lane by the time he reached the cottage door. He looked inside but could see no one there. Perhaps the girl was hiding somewhere beyond the garden. Perhaps she was in a secret place, a place like the forest, where everything was quiet and she could be on her own.

Slowly Bethsany and Maben walked up the hill. Where the road parted three ways, they began another less steep climb along the muddy trackway which led to the stream and open grasslands beyond. As the ground levelled off, Maben began to run, his thin frame twisting and jumping as the forest came into view. This was his home, not the stables in the castle or the dark rooms of the old woman's cottage, but here, this open stretch of land which lay high above the town, between the silver stream and the mystery of the great trees.

'Maben!'

Bethsany called him to heel. He was drifting too far from their dwelling. But something had caught Maben's attention. He stopped. There, on the threshold of the forest, he could see two figures – Elowen and the boy from the castle who they called Kettleby.

(iii)

Dan Arent slouched against the gaol wall looking up at the barred opening that sat level with the street. Occasionally he glimpsed the shoes and ankles of a passer-by. He yawned, stretched his shoulders. His first night of his new term in gaol had been long, cold, and uncomfortable.

Three other men occupied Arent's cell – newcomers, who'd come to port on board one of the many trade ships that helped feed the town and make a good profit for local merchants. They were hard-boiled sailors, Dutch and French, arrested after a night's drinking and brawling. All three were asleep on the dusty gaol floor. Did they even notice, Arent wondered, that the town had been requisitioned by the English parliament's army? He smiled. It hardly seemed to matter. Men went about their business regardless of who ruled. There would always be stout town burghers with sharp elbows willing to turn a penny into a shilling, regardless of whether Fairfax or old man Arundell was in charge.

A key turned in the lock. Two soldiers entered – young, uncertain – brandishing pistols. One called out Arent's name whereupon the Dutchman's wrists were cuffed and he was ordered to walk out of his cell into an ante-room situated along a corridor. Inside, a familiar looking man in uniform sat at a table, writing on a piece of parchment: Colonel Fortescue.

'You are beginning to test my patience, Captain Arent.'

'I can explain ...'

'I sincerely hope that you can. The last time our paths crossed, I was generous in my dealings. This time I will not be so.' Fortescue, his quill delicately poised, ended his correspondence with a brisk flourish. He looked up. 'Your blatant disregard to leave English soil is a serious offence. Parliament will not shirk in its duty to protect this land from seditious activity.'

'I have a document, sir, which I would like you to read. I have kept it safe about my person. May I?' He bent down and took out the crumpled letter from where it was hidden in his boot, then offered it, despite his cuffed wrists, to Fortescue. The colonel hesitated before accepting it with an impatient look.

'What is it?' the colonel asked, unfolding the letter.

'I was asked to deliver it to the governor of Pendennis Castle. Your intervention, sir, prevented me from doing so.'

Fortescue began to read. As he did so, Arent said, 'I was ready to board ship with my crew, so as to comply with your ruling; yet I felt in my heart duty-bound to deliver this letter in person.'

'Did you not think to hand it to one of my officers, Captain?'

Arent hesitated. 'Yes, I did, sir. But I could not be sure it would make its way into the hands of the governor. There is terrible suffering within the castle.'

Fortescue lay the parchment before him. 'Suffering of the governor's own making, Captain. Arundell is an aged fool. We have offered generous terms of surrender.'

'But it is precisely because he believes relief is on its way that he continues with his stubbornness. He must be made aware that no help is forthcoming.'

Fortescue turned the letter once again, read each line quickly, derision in his eyes.

'I will see to it that the contents of the letter are made known to the castle's Council of War. You will remain in the gaol until such time as arrangements can be made to transport you from this place. Remove him.'

The two soldiers stepped forward.

'Wait! Please. I beg you, Colonel. There is more I should tell!' Arent said.

Fortescue waved his hand. 'Enough, Captain Arent!'

The lead soldier took hold of Arent's arm. Arent snatched it away. 'I must speak with you on another matter, regarding the Prince of Wales's carriage.'

As Arent expected, his words took hold of the colonel's attention. Fortescue indicated that the soldiers step back from the prisoner.

'What do you know, Captain Arent, of the prince's carriage?'

As Fortescue awaited an answer, Arent became aware that he needed to choose his words carefully.

'I know that a chest was being carried, a chest filled with treasure which the young prince was about to trade for arms and men. I, sir, am now in possession of the chest.'

Fortescue's demeanour hardened as if he, too, were reluctant to play a full hand. 'Perhaps you could explain to me how this chest came into your possession?'

'By default, sir. It was discovered buried in a forest. The chest bears the Prince of Wales's emblem.'

'And what else does this royal chest "bear"?'

'Riches,' Arent said. 'Riches beyond all reason; riches that would buy an army and more besides.'

There followed a silence between them. Fortescue rose from his desk, shuffled a pace or two, collecting his thoughts. 'And what is it you seek, Captain Arent, in exchange for this chest that you claim once belonged to the Prince of Wales?'

Arent, surprised by the Colonel's forthright tone, said, 'My ship, sir – fully restored and made ready to sail. And the delivery of the letter in order that the siege might be ended. I seek nothing more, nothing less.'

Fortescue nodded. 'And if the chest is a fake?'

Arent smiled. 'You will not find it to be so; I give you my word.'

Whether the colonel was content with this proposition,

Arent wasn't certain. Fortescue looked suddenly weary now; the suspicion in his eyes had slipped away and Arent wondered if he had been counting on another outcome with regard to the royal chest, or whether he had even known of its existence. It was only when Fortescue ordered the soldiers to free Arent of his shackles that he realised Fortescue's dilemma: to keep the chest safe in anticipation of the return to the throne of the king, or to hand it over to Parliament. It was a gamble either way – a gamble that might decide Fortescue's fate once the fighting was over. Such were the choices, thought Arent, offered up by this brutal and petty English civil war.

22.

(i)

There was quiet apprehension between Ann, Bethsany and the others as they waited upon Arent's return. Cadwaller spent the morning showing Maben how to shape wood with a knife; Kettleby helped Elowen with the daily chores. Ann stood gazing anxiously in the direction of the pathway that led to the town, hopeful of seeing the Dutch captain striding towards her.

At mid-day, when they had finished cleaning the chicken coop, Elowen and Kettleby announced they would go to the forest. Kettleby, who had been sheltered in his youth from trapping and butchery, wanted to help Elowen recover her prey. Maben stared at the former ensign with steely eyes.

Ann told them to wait. She went indoors and prepared a small basket of goods for Elijah — bread, cakes, mutton and the cider apples Bethsany had procured from market. She handed the basket to Kettleby.

'Stay and talk awhile,' she said, 'and let him know of your adventures.'

She watched as they ambled across the grasslands. Elowen beckoned Gallant to join them. The old dog had been waiting outside her grandmother's dwelling, whining and with a lost look in his rheumy eyes, as if expecting the old woman to reappear. Elowen called again. Slowly Gallant stood, shook himself out, and followed, head down, in their wake.

Elowen showed Kettleby the different pathways through the forest. They walked first in the direction of the road, before criss-crossing and making their way towards Elijah's dwelling. They would not go near the footman's decomposed body – Elowen would not allow Kettleby to know about that. She would start with the traps farthest away, then follow her set route as she had done with the boy.

Gallant whined; Elowen, impatient, ignored the dog's cries and encouraged him to wander free.

Kettleby stood like an inquisitive schoolboy as Elowen knelt beside her traps; he leaned in with a curious eye as she snapped the necks of the plump squirrels, rabbits, and pigeons she found therein. He followed her at a moderate pace, holding the hunting sack as well as the basket for Elijah.

'You are so skilled, Elowen,' he told her. 'So knowledgeable about the nature of the world. It is as if you have been hewn from the very trees, the leaves and the soil.'

She didn't know what to say in reply to his ramblings, so she said nothing. His life had been spent within a secure, cultured family – something that Elowen would never know.

As they walked towards Elijah's dwelling, they heard Gallant's mournful whine. The old dog was sniffing the pots, pieces of wood, discarded furniture and panels that were too cumbersome to be kept inside.

'Away!' said Elowen as she neared the rickety house.

Gallant whined again and spread himself flat on the ground.

It was then that Elowen realised: the old dog was acting in the same manner as when her grandmother had passed from this life. Elowen had been away too long, had lost her ability to sense the subtle changes of things. Sure enough, having motioned to Kettleby that all was not as it should be, they entered the ramshackle building and discovered Elijah at peace in his bed. The old man looked as though he was sleeping – his face brushed with wry contentment.

'You knew him for many years?' Kettleby said, uneasy before death's sudden intrusion.

'Yes,' said Elowen. 'Since I was a child. Elijah taught me many things.'

'I'm sorry, Elowen, and so soon after your grandmother was taken.'

Elowen covered Elijah's face. 'The old folk from these parts are no longer among us.' Once again, the atmosphere of the day had turned.

(ii)

Cadwaller and Kettleby dug Elijah's grave on the edge of the forest, close to the old man's dwelling. Ann and Bethsany washed the body, then wrapped it in the blanket Elijah used in his bed. Using the money Bethsany saved from the market, Elowen took a measurement of the corpse and set off with Kettleby to the coffin maker. They returned with a plain rectangular box in which the old man could be laid. Cadwaller knocked the top several times with his knuckle, criticising the soft, thin wood the undertaker had used, saying it was of little use and would not bear a body underground for long.

When Elijah had been placed inside and the lid nailed into place, Ann gave thanks for the old man's life. She recounted his days at sea, spoke well of him as a neighbour and friend. They sang a hymn and lowered the box into the ground. Then Cadwaller, Elowen and Kettleby began to shovel the earth.

That evening, they dug a fire pit and sat together, feasting on mutton broth, bread and the cider that Elijah kept for those nights he sat alone beneath the stars. Cadwaller lightened the mood with the tale of how he provoked Irish Tom on the wharf so that Arent was able to slip quietly away.

'I tried to whisper to Tom as we were having our set-to that it was all just a merry ruse so that our captain could flee. But Tom's a bit slow between the ears; he was cuffing me left, right and centre! But the worst of it was when he threw me in the brine; that left me thinking, as I flailed about in the harbour, that if I managed to crawl out, he'd only go and cuff me again! So, I held myself fast beneath the wharf, takin' advantage of all the mayhem that was goin' on; and then, when they'd all gone, I swam further along the shore. I heaved myself onto a slip of land – sodden I was, like a half-drowned ferret – and took refuge in a shed that was used for guttin' fish. Fortescue's men must have been desperate to see the back of our crew 'cause they didn't try all that hard to find me! Once our men had boarded, they gave the order to set sail.'

Kettleby and Elowen found Cadwaller's story a hearty relief, laughing as the cloudy cider worked its magic. Bethsany, though, sat quiet beside Maben, as was her usual nature, attending to the boy's manners as he ate, tapping his hands if he took more than was good for him. Meanwhile, Ann's thoughts seemed to be elsewhere; she smiled and told Cadwaller that he was a rare fellow who had helped many from the castle escape that day when the shelling rained down. But she seemed tired and wary of what the morning might bring, glancing sideways every so often, waiting on the return of Dan Arent.

The fire burned down, and the night winds began to drive across the grasslands. The group set their bowls and spoons in a bucket in order that Maben might do his duty and scuttle down to the stream and wash them out. Then, when the cold was too much to bear, they gave a final toast to Elijah before retiring to their beds.

(iii)

Arent, too, was dining that night, with Fortescue at Arwenack Manor. He sat opposite the colonel in the long room at a neatly set table, staring at a beef dinner served on silver plate. One of Fortescue's orderlies poured Arent a glass of burgundy and Fortescue raised his glass.

'To new beginnings, Captain,' he said.

Arent nodded and took a generous draught. Then he waited for the final interrogation to begin.

'We were aware of the Prince of Wales's carriage coming to grief,' said Fortescue. 'News travels quick in these parts.'

Arent chewed a tender piece of beef. 'Do you know what happened to halt the carriage's progress?'

'Our agents seem to think that there were two drivers and

a single footman. When the carriage's wheel became stricken, the drivers used three of the horses to transport the prince with a two-man guard to Pendennis Castle.'

'And the footman?'

'Left behind, until the drivers' return. Only it seems that he was tempted by the chest and its contents. A considerable sum was – is – housed therein. He succumbed to temptation, unable to resist the lure of the king's treasure.'

Arent took another draught of wine. As he did so, the young orderly entered to stoke the fire. A subtle gesture ensued from Fortescue, and Arent's glass was filled once more to its brim.

'You believe, then,' said Arent, 'that the footman buried the chest in the forest in order to retrieve it at a later date?'

Fortescue dabbed his lips with a napkin. 'That would be the most logical explanation, Mr Arent. But my officers made a search of the area and discovered something that would suggest an altogether different train of events.'

Arent laid down his knife and fork. *Be careful with your words,* he thought, *lest you implicate Elowen and the boy.* 'They discovered something inside the abandoned carriage?'

Fortescue shook his head. 'By this time the carriage was gone, Mr Arent. The locals had taken it for themselves. They scavenge from those ships that have been scuttled on the rocks; it is only natural, therefore, that they scavenge along the roads as well. No – my officers discovered another small ditch, situated only a few feet away from the carriage, a ditch that was big enough for a king's chest to be buried.'

Arent considered this. 'May I suggest there is a simple

explanation, Colonel?'

'Let me hear of it.'

Arent took a breath. 'The footman first saw fit to bury the chest close by the carriage in order to wait for his fellow drivers to return.'

'How so? He intended to steal it!'

'Think of it, Colonel. You are alone on a country road, entrusted with keeping safe the king's chest. What if you are set upon by a band of rogues? The chest would be hidden. The footman's loyalty was well thought out.'

Fortescue pondered over this explanation as the orderly cleared their plates. 'But tell me, Arent, by what magic did the chest come to shift into the forest?'

'The footman's greed proved too much. Instead of keeping the chest buried near the road, and remaining loyal to the king, he reclaimed it and dragged it into the forest, where he buried it for a second time, in order to return.'

'Or, perhaps he *was* set upon by rogues, who in turn hid the royal treasure.'

'And the footman?'

'Killed – and his body spirited away.'

Arent baulked at this suggestion. Had Elowen killed the footman? It disturbed him to think on it. And then what had happened when the drivers returned? It wasn't beyond reason to believe that they were the culprits. Or else, scared beyond their wits at the footman's treason, they shed their uniforms and ran away to save themselves from the suspicion that would surely have followed.

'It is a mystery, Mr Arent,' said Fortescue with a sigh. 'We will speak some more of it after we have slept. You will stay here the night as my guest; then, at dawn, I will follow you and recover the chest on behalf of Parliament.'

'What of my ship?'

The two men rose from their chairs. 'I am a man of my word, Captain. On delivery of the chest, you will be free to take the helm of the *Adventurer* and return to your home.'

They shook hands. The orderly showed Arent to his room. His time in Cornwall was nearing its end. And a moment of sadness passed over the Dutchman as he thought of the new friends he was about to lose.

(iv)

A sharp knock on the door roused Arent at first light. Fortescue and a handful of his men were already standing in the courtyard as the horses were being prepared.

'I trust you slept well, Captain,' said Fortescue. Arent said he did. 'Good. Let us hope this matter will soon be resolved to our mutual satisfaction. Arundell has once again refused terms and now lives on borrowed time. An afternoon sally of canon might be needed to heave the old wretch to his senses.'

There was a rippling of laughter from the troops. They mounted their horses and Fortescue told Arent to lead the way. The Dutchman detected a harder edge in the colonel's attitude from the previous night. Whether this was merely a tactic, allowing the commander to ingratiate himself with his troops, or something more, Arent wasn't sure. As they rode out from the grounds of Arwenack Manor, a more disturbing thought crossed his mind: that Fortescue had received new orders from London telling him to confiscate the royal chest and return the Dutch captain to his gaol.

Falmouth town, like Rotterdam harbour, was alive at this early hour. Ships were putting to sail and fishing boats were jostling to land their catch. In the market square, sellers were laying out their wares. Only the gaol looked shuttered and lifeless – filled, no doubt, with more sleeping ne'er-do-wells from the night before. Everyone, Arent noted, cast a sly glance at the group riding in the direction of the steep hill that led out of town.

As they ascended the rising road, passing the lane where Bethsany took Maben to visit the old woman and the girl, Arent noticed other prying eyes looking out from the tiny dwellings that straggled the hill. Fortescue rode beside him while the four other riders remained in close formation behind, rod-straight in their saddles. As they reached the crest of the hill, Arent indicated the hidden pathway shrouded by trees.

'This is the route I take,' he said. 'I do not know of any other.'

Fortescue dismounted and peered into the dark, narrow pathway. 'How long to walk, Captain?' he asked.

'Fifteen-twenty minutes at a brisk pace,' said Arent. The colonel turned to his troops. He ordered two of them to remain with the horses. The colonel, Arent, and the others would continue on foot.

Fortescue was surprised to see that dwellings existed in such an isolated part of the town. As they walked across the open grassland, he pointed to Elijah's shack and asked who it was that lived there. Arent told him that the dwelling was in bad repair.

'It is inhabited by an old one-legged man,' he said. But Fortescue's interest had been stirred sufficiently for him to ask further questions regarding the size of the dwelling and its capacity for expansion, leading Arent to wonder, rather uneasily, if he was marking it as a place to billet troops.

Gallant appeared and bounded towards the Dutchman, licking his hands and jumping up onto hind legs in a grand gesture of affection.

'It seems that you are well known here and well liked,' said Fortescue.

At that moment, Arent saw Ann and Bethsany emerge from their dwelling. As the group neared them, he hoped that Cadwaller, Elowen, and Kettleby had made themselves scarce and were not available for interrogation as to how they came upon the chest.

'Mr Arent, thank the Lord you are safe and well.'

It was Ann who spoke. The wan complexion and disturbed demeanour that had coloured her time at the castle had now abated. Her face was once again fresh and clear, her eyes sparkling with the faith that Arent had feared was about to desert her.

'I have been in receipt of Colonel Fortescue's hospitality, Mistress,' he said. 'I hope my absence did not give you cause for alarm.'

Fortescue introduced himself. 'Captain Arent has brought me here in order to conclude some urgent business. I trust the royal chest has remained safe in your keeping.'

Ann said that the chest remained as they found it.

'Then let us go to it,' said Fortescue, and Arent escorted him into the small stone building.

The colonel marvelled at the treasure, holding up pieces of silver plate, allowing diamond-studded trinkets to sit gently in the palm of his hand. He reasoned that the treasure's worth was enough to purchase a substantial fighting force. 'And let us not mistake the king's intention,' he said. 'It is to land such a force in Cornwall and blight the county with even more destruction.'

Arent shifted uncomfortably as the colonel toyed with the glistening trinkets. His eyes flickered towards Ann who responded with subtle glances, indicating that there was nothing to fear. When Fortescue finally decided that he seen enough, he locked the chest and ordered his troopers to carry it back to the waiting horses. He shook Arent's hand.

'I will issue instructions that the *Adventurer* be docked at the wharf. From tomorrow morning she will once again be in your hands. Prepare her for sail, Mr Arent, and take your leave. I wish you good fortune.'

When the colonel had gone Arent turned to Ann. 'Where are they?'

She smiled. 'Elowen and Maben were tasked to watch the road leading from town. As soon as they spied you and the colonel, they returned and sounded the alarm.'

'Does the lord turn a blind eye to such trickery, Mistress?'

'Only when it is put to good use, Captain,' said Ann, and Arent laughed. He took Ann's hand and put it to his lips, causing Bethsany to flinch with embarrassment, whereupon Arent took hold of her hand, too, and did the same.

It didn't take long for Cadwaller, Elowen, Kettleby and Maben to emerge from the forest. The news that Fortescue had taken the chest and the *Adventurer* was to be returned to its rightful owner was the cause of much joy. Ann said that the safe return of the ship's captain was the thing that most warmed her heart.

They feasted again that evening – chicken, fish and barley bread – with much discussion of future plans. Cadwaller said that he yearned to see his wife and children.

'She is much younger than I,' he explained, 'and the children are hard to handle. I will see to it that she is well rewarded for her patience. It is a hard lot being a seafarer's wife, that's for sure.'

Kettleby said that he would return to his parents' house in Penzance. 'And I have invited Elowen to travel with me, if she can stand being away from her traps!'

Ann and Bethsany said little. Their lives had always been lived within the confines of the forest and the town. They had no plans for such grand adventures – faith in God and the salvation of the boy Maben were their goals.

'And what plans do you harbour, Captain?' said Ann, alive with the heat from the flickering fire.

'My plan is a simple one,' he said. 'Fixed on a straight course that will not waver, a plan that Cadwaller knows well and does not entirely agree with. I intend to make a new life in the East Indies. And I would be honoured, Mistress Ann, if you would consider joining me there.'

23.

(i)

On the 15th August, old governor Arundell finally capitulated. Informed by Fortescue that the Prince of Wales's treasure chest had been recovered, he begrudgingly accepted that no army from afar was about to land and re-take Cornwall for the king. Even so, it took a delegation, comprising his son Richard, Major General Molesworth, Sir Abraham Shipman and a sergeant of the guard to fully explain the extreme desperation of the castle's inhabitants. Desertions had become commonplace; rations, now cut by two-thirds, had dramatically increased the mortality rate among women and children.

'Fortescue has offered generous terms,' said Richard Arundell. 'To refuse is to bring upon the garrison horrors the like of which this county has not seen for a hundred and more years.'

Sir John irritably waved his hand at his son, indicating quiet. He was standing at the window, looking down onto the parade ground. Outside, a good number of the flimsy shelters, their occupants now buried near the stables, had collapsed, the wind dispersing wood and sack cloth across the square into the bleakest corners of the castle's buildings and walls. Few soldiers paced the battlements; those that did stood weak, shivering. And even Arundell had noticed that night beacons, which served as a symbol of the castle's resistance, were no longer being lit. The old governor turned, his cheeks red as berries, contempt in his eyes. Then, in a voice that was feeble and yet defiant, he ordered his council of war to accept Fortescue's terms of surrender.

Now the decision had been made, there was much to do. Richard Arundell issued an order that the garrison make itself ready to depart. There was no formal announcement of the governor's decision, no mention of surrender relayed to the starving wretches who had endured months of torment. Those that were able were told to gather what they could; others, too sickly to contemplate marching out with heads held high, were left to accept whatever fate had in hand. In the governor's quarters, Sir John steadfastly refused to leave by the castle's moated entrance, demanding a boat be made ready for him to sail directly to his grand house in Trerice. He knew full well that news travelled fast in the town. Old Jack for the king would not run the gauntlet of the hostile crowds that were certain to gather along the castle road, armed with rotten fruit and fish guts. He would leave Shipman and Molesworth with the thankless task of leading out the remnants of the garrison. Father and son would escape through the south gate, to plot Parliament's fall anew.

*

The news of the surrender did indeed travel quickly. No sooner had Fortescue's officers delivered the signed parchment of capitulation to Arwenack Manor than it seemed the town's population had been furnished with the requisite information. Declarations were shouted in the town square:

'The castle ha' surrendered! I tell 'ee, as God be my witness – the castle ha' surrendered!' Cheering, tears and disbelief rang out; it was as if the war between Parliament and the king itself had come to a sudden end.

Such was the commotion that Bethsany nearly toppled backwards in her chair.

'Maben, boy – here!' she shouted after she had righted herself with assistance from one of the market boys. 'Gather up our wares – we must home, d'reckly. See to it, boy, see to it!'

They hurried up the hill, passing by the lane where the cottage and the girl could be found, for which Maben was thankful. And when they reached their dwelling, they found Ann sitting outside with Arent before the fire pit, deep in conversation – a conversation that ended abruptly when they were told of the end of the siege.

Arent especially was thankful that it was over. Pindar's letter remained in his knapsack – a souvenir for him now to take home – and he closed his eyes for a short while in meditation at the role he had played. And when Kettleby, Elowen and Cadwaller emerged from the forest, Ann gathered them together to tell them the joyous news before leading a prayer of thanks for the lives that had been saved.

'Will you join us, Captain?' she said as a circle was formed.

It had been many years since Arent stood in prayer. Yet he nodded his assent and took his place with the others, enjoying Ann's voice which was soothing and firm and wise to his ears. Afterwards, Arent and Cadwaller made their way into the town to check on the *Adventurer* and see for themselves the defeated garrison march out of Pendennis.

(ii)

When Arent and Cadwaller had gone, Ann was overcome by a feeling of loneliness. She could not understand why she felt this way; it seemed strange to her that such a feeling would present itself immediately after Captain Arent's leave-taking. At supper, she ate little and excused herself from the table, telling Bethsany and Maben that the excitement of the castle's surrender had made her lose her appetite. She took on her cape and said that she yearned to be alone and left them for a while to take in the evening air.

She passed by the dwelling in which Elowen and Kettleby were resting before making her way to the threshold of the forest. Arent had left her confused after his ridiculous pronouncement that he wished her to sail on the *Adventurer* with him to the tropics. How dare he! Did he really think she would leave Cornwall, her home, for an unknown place on the other side of the world? Why, she had Bethsany and Maben to take care of; and there were the members of her church – poor, humble folk who looked to her for guidance. Who else among them would stand in the village square preaching the word of the Lord? How he, Mr Arent, a man she had only known for a small number of weeks, expected her to give serious consideration to such an offer – on a ship recently impounded by Parliament – was nothing but downright impertinence. There was good in him, yes, she had to admit. He had striven to rescue Maben and had proved the innocent were close to his heart. Yet, it was unbecoming for him to make such overtures towards her. Her life followed another, distinct course.

She stopped suddenly, realising that she had walked much further into the forest than she had intended. In her deliberations, she had wandered along the faint trackway that led to Elijah's dwelling. She turned and began to walk back towards the open grassland accordingly. She had heard of the place Arent spoke about – the East Indies – from fellow members of her congregation, former merchant traders who dealt in spices, textiles and yarn. And she had been told of the men and women of faith who spread the word of the Lord, creating new congregations among people who had laboured under primitive religions, bringing them into Christ's arms. With her temper now more even, Ann wondered about this yearning to preach in far-off worlds. Was that her true calling? Had God sent Captain Dan Arent into her life to lead her along a new path?

As she crossed the forest threshold, a late burst of afternoon sun shone through the clouds as if to clarify her torment. No, she thought, she could never consider it. God had placed her here, high above the town, with her sister and the boy touched by the moon. It was settled: she would decline Captain Arent's offer.

(iii)

Dan Arent and Cadwaller Jones stood at the crest of the hill road leading to Pendennis Castle. They were among a throng of people waiting for members of the stricken garrison to emerge. Many who stood alongside Arent and Cadwaller were relatives, uncertain if their loved ones were alive or dead. The mood was one of uncertainty and resignation. Times were strange; ordinary folk's lives, it was said, were being rolled around in a barrel full of nails.

Before the castle's entrance, a troop of Fortescue's cavalry assembled. In accordance with the terms of surrender, they took up position, ready to lead the garrison towards Arwenack Manor. There, after laying down arms, a formal surrender was to be offered, after which each member of the garrison would be given a shilling before being told to disperse.

'Generous,' said Cadwaller, his eyes fixed on Fortescue's troop of horse. 'A garrison that refuses to surrender for six months can usually expect the sword and nothin' less.'

Arent, weary of all the violence he'd seen, remained quiet. He turned and looked down across the harbour. From his vantage point he could see clusters of ships moored near the wharf. He tried to pick out the *Adventurer* but his eyes struggled to focus and he again wondered if Fortescue was about to break his word.

'They're comin',' Cadwaller said.

Fortescue's cavalrymen were trying to calm their horses as a flourish of pipes and drums sounded from within the castle's grounds. The brisk trilling and the heavy thumps grew ever louder until the cavalry horses, growing impatient, were slowly reined-in and driven downhill. When the remnants of the garrison emerged, the crowd began to murmur – a strange mix of anger, shock and compassion. The column was led by Major General Molesworth and Sir Abraham Shipman, followed by the castle's officers. They marched with heads high, their eyes unwavering in their desire to avoid looking at the crowd. Behind the officers came a ragged mix of soldiers, wives and children, faces etched with terror at what awaited them, the brutality of siege apparent by the stubbornness of their despair.

Arent and Cadwaller watched nearly seven hundred broken souls from Pendennis Castle pass them by. Another two hundred – too weak or injured to follow the garrison to freedom – lay abandoned on the parade ground. Within the castle walls, hurrying past the rubble of the stables and skirting the burial mounds, Sir John Arundell and his son Richard headed towards the southern gate, and to a skiff waiting to ferry them to safety.

*

Afterwards, Arent and Cadwaller walked through the town to the wharf. There, tied ready for departure, lay the *Adventurer*. Arent sighed with relief; Fortescue had kept his word.

Cadwaller slapped Arent on the back. 'Well done, Captain,' he said. 'In two days, we'll be home and I'll have a wife and three young scamps to put up with.'

'I still intend to make my way to the East Indies, Cadwaller. My mind hasn't changed on account of what has happened to us.'

'As you wish,' Cadwaller said. 'If that's the long and short of it … I can always find work trapping rats or netting birds …'

Arent ignored his friend's pathetic attempt at gaining sympathy. 'I've asked Mistress Ann to accompany me,' he said. 'There's been no answer, but I'm hopeful she will look kindly on my offer.'

They reached the gangplank where they stood awhile, each

awaiting the other to cross onto the ship's deck.

'And what are your intentions towards her, Captain?' said Cadwaller. 'It'll take more than an offer of a sea crossing to entice her. She has her sister and the boy to care for, an' a church congregation to keep on the side. I fear your offer will fall short.'

As they made their way on deck, Arent began to speculate about whether his friend was correct. The idea of a proposal of marriage was something he had considered; but a damning voice infected him whenever he did so, a voice that reminded him of the sanctity of his bond to his late wife. He said no more about it to Cadwaller and his friend went about checking the ship as if the conversation had never happened. They examined the main sail and the rigging, then prepared to wash down the decking.

'Here,' said Cadwaller, throwing Arent an old broom. As he did so, three familiar figures appeared on the wharf.

'Can we come on board, Captain? We're willing to lend a hand if needed.'

Arent beckoned them towards him. Thomas Kettleby, Elowen and the boy, Maben.

(iv)

It was the first time Kettleby, Elowen and Maben had stepped aboard a ship. They walked slowly from one end to the other, gazing at the masts, peering overboard and into the galley as if they had stumbled into a strange new world of wonderment.

'An' this 'ere's where the captain and his mate steer her

through the calm and the rough,' said Cadwaller, enjoying his moment as chief guide. He set Maben behind the big wheel and the boy took hold of it with both hands. 'Steer due east, scamp,' said Cadwaller, 'home to Rotterdam!' Kettleby and Elowen laughed while Arent scoured the wharf, as if expecting Ann and Bethsany to appear.

Then it was all hands to the pump to make the *Adventurer* ready for her voyage home. The deck was swilled and brushed, the sails checked, the galley cleaned. Arent unfurled a rope ladder to assess the outside of the hull; Cadwaller, crawling on hands and knees in the bilges, prodded the timbers with his knife, Maben scurrying close behind.

The bustle of the wharf was constant. Fishermen and sailors for hire enquired about Arent's plans. He told them that he'd be setting sail next day, bound for Rotterdam; after that, he couldn't say with certainty. The ship would either be sold or else bound for the Dutch East Indies. To those who were interested in taking passage to Rotterdam, he said they should make themselves known tomorrow.

'It'll be a mid-day sailing, on high tide,' he said.

It was late afternoon when the work was done and they made their way to Ann and Bethsany's dwelling. As he climbed the hill to the open grasslands, Maben running ahead, Kettleby, Elowen and Cadwaller in good humour behind, Arent felt a heady thrum of anticipation, as if a new beginning was about to be salvaged from the folly of Pindar's mission. Arent would ask Ann for her answer; despite what Cadwaller had said, he was confident in her desire to accept.

24.

(i)

The table had been laid. A pot of fish soup was steaming on the hearth. Dark bread and cheese, purchased from the market, had been cut and set on a platter ready to eat. Since Elijah had passed away, Bethsany had taken to pressing apples and she offered each guest a cup of thick, cloudy cider.

'To friendship,' said Arent raising his cup, which, they all agreed, was a fine toast to make.

Arent kept a tender eye on Ann, awaiting his moment. She went about the business of serving dinner quietly and efficiently, avoiding Arent's gaze.

'There's news to tell,' said Cadwaller, raising his already excitable voice. 'There's a full crew a'ready for us tomorrow, Captain.' Arent, caught unawares by this sudden development, asked Cadwaller to stop speaking in riddles and to speak plain. He knew of only four men who had enquired about taking passage with the *Adventurer*, men whose abilities left much to be desired.

'They're sitting here with us now, Captain – it'll be Elowen and Kettleby that's ready to make good the sails an' help guide us home.'

Arent, Ann and Bethsany turned to the young couple.

'We wish to sail with you tomorrow, Captain Arent, if there's place aboard,' said Elowen. Her words dampened the business of their meal until only an uneasy silence prevailed. It was Bethsany who broke it as she scooped portions of soup into their bowls and asked Ann to say grace.

'Well, well,' said Arent when they were all done and had eagerly set about their meal. 'The young turtledoves wish to see Rotterdam.'

'And more, Captain,' Kettleby said. 'Much more. We will voyage to the Indies and feel the warmth of the sun on our backs, too.'

Arent looked towards Ann who felt impelled to comment. 'So, you have put aside your desire to go home to Penzance?'

He nodded. 'Yes, Mistress. Elowen and I have decided to seek pastures new."

Kettleby placed his upturned hand next to Elowen's; she gripped his hand in return.

'Then we wish you well, dear Elowen and Kettleby,' Ann said. 'You will both be missed in these parts. But I am certain that, God willing, one day you will both return.'

The meal passed mostly in silence. Even Cadwaller, enthused by the prospect of the *Adventurer* at last setting off for home, could feel tension between Arent and Ann, as well as Ann's mild displeasure towards Elowen and Kettleby.

Maben, slurping his soup not quite in the way the good Lord intended, had his hand slapped by Bethsany.

Arent looked around: there was unfinished business to attend to and not many hours left with which to bring it to a conclusion.

When their bowls were empty and Bethsany was preparing stewed fruit, Ann went outside with scraps for Gallant. Arent excused himself from table and followed her.

'Mistress Ann – is all well with you?'

Ann knelt and attended to the hound who, excited by the rich scent of his meal, nuzzled his head against her long skirt. 'I am as well as can be expected, Captain Arent,' she answered in a cool manner.

'I was hoping, Mistress, that you might have given some thought to the suggestion that I put to you.'

Gallant ate greedily. Ann stood straight. 'It is not possible for me to voyage from here, Captain. Only short minutes ago I was told of dear Elowen's plans to leave this place. Who will be left to guide Maben and my sister if I decide to travel half-way across the world?'

Arent took a step towards her, encouraging a guarded intimacy. The evening was still warm, and the sound of the running stream seemed to invite a thousand new opportunities.

'Then bring Bethsany and the boy. There is a better life awaiting, a life in which war can be cast aside in honour of the greater glory of God.'

A flicker of her eyes at that moment told the truth of her; she wavered between what she had known all her life and a chance to break from it. What, he wondered, was she scared of? What was it that held her so tightly here? The rugged coast that had forged her faith? The people who lived in poverty and to whom she ministered in the town square?

'I cannot,' she said. 'Please, Captain Arent – if you wish to honour our friendship, do not press me any further. My place is here among our people who I value and who value me in return.'

She swept past him then, and entered her dwelling, leaving Arent alone with just the sound of the stream and Gallant's busy eating to listen to. He had failed; and now he felt that his invitation to Ann had been a mistake. He had sought comfort in the presence of another and was left with a familiar feeling that haunted him wherever he went – the deep, unfathomable sadness that he felt having turned, however briefly, away from the memory of his wife and children.

(ii)

After the meal, Arent and Cadwaller walked back to the wharf and slept on board the *Adventurer* for the first time in many weeks. Arent said nothing about Ann's refusal and Cadwaller, sensing his friend's unhappiness, didn't ask about the conversation that had taken place when Ann went to give Gallant the dog his supper.

Arent slept fitfully in his bunk, waking every two hours, the gentle rocking of the ship and the night sounds of the wharf unfamiliar to him after his time living near the forest. Ann's refusal also played on his mind; and his wife, when she appeared in his dreams, sometimes angry, sometimes consoling, seemed to mirror Arent's hopes and fears for the future. In the early hours he got up and went to the victual cupboard; he poured out the last of the rum and gulped it down in one, searching for a promise of peace before he left Falmouth and Cornwall forever.

The rum did its job; he woke to the rattling sound of someone turning the handle on his door. It was Cadwaller who roused him. There were men on the wharf, he said, new men with experience who wished to board and work their passage. And there were other things for him to attend to before they could slip their mooring and sail.

Arent dressed, went on deck, ready for whatever the day threw at him.

'Are you well, Captain?' shouted Cadwaller. Arent smiled and waved. It was nine fifteen in the morning; they would depart that afternoon.

After taking his pick of crew, Arent was then obliged to decide on a group of locals who wished to sail as fee paying passengers. Some were royalists, unconvinced by the new regime that was emerging in England. Rotterdam would be their entry point to Europe and a new life amongst the loyal exiles who had gathered overseas in hope of seeing Charles retake his place on the throne. Arent didn't care much for these people but as long as they had money to pay he ushered them on board. Only the very drunk and the very poor were rejected, despite Fortescue's troops, who wished to see the back of any ne'er-do-well in the town, willing them along the gangplank.

At mid-day, Elowen and Kettleby appeared. Arent embraced them both.

'It stirs my heart that you will be joining us,' he said.

How much their lives had changed in the space of these few months he thought. Elowen's hair had grown again to shoulder length; her complexion was full, her eyes eager and alert. The stresses of the castle siege and the curse of the devil were in the past. And, of course, there was Kettleby – tall, gangling, rake-thin, once of a nervous disposition, but whose worship of the girl had transformed him into a courteous young man with a clear vision of the future.

'And what of Mistress Ann and Bethsany and the boy, Maben?' said Arent. 'Are they not here to wave you farewell?'

'They are in the town square, at market,' Kettleby said. 'They will not come to the wharf. They fear it will tear at their hearts to witness our departure.'

With the crew and passengers chosen and the *Adventurer's* sails made ready, Arent cast a final look over the wharf. Cadwaller called out from the wheel deck. 'She's good to sail, Captain.' Arent nodded and, after accepting that Ann was lost to him, gave the order for the gangplank to be taken away.

(iii)

When he spoke with Arent upon boarding the *Adventurer* Kettleby did not adequately highlight the turmoil Ann Netherton had felt following her conversation with the Dutch Captain the previous night. After their dinner and Arent and Cadwaller's leave-taking, she too had struggled to sleep. Her mind raced with conflicting thoughts about her life, about her loyalties, about her faith. But she thought mostly of Arent. He intrigued her, she realised; she saw in him something of herself. And she had feelings for him, she had to admit — feelings that she had never before experienced for a man. Perhaps it was to do with his rejection of God, the idea that salvation could be reversed, given up for a life of non-belief. Was there a wound — a lesion — to be found in her soul as well? An unknown wound that was, even now, making her waver?

When next morning she left their dwelling with Bethsany and Maben, she determined that she could not stand on the wharf and wave the *Adventurer* goodbye. It would be too difficult for her to witness. So, upon arriving in the town, she blessed Elowen and Kettleby in the market square and said a prayer, asking God to guide them in all that they did. Elowen kissed Maben's forehead and urged him to be godly in his manners and aspect. She also told him that her animal traps were now entrusted to him. He had been a fine helpmate, Elowen said; now it was time for Maben to work alone.

Bethsany gave them a basket of food for their voyage. Kettleby offered his hand to Maben who slapped it with his palm in a strange demonstration of anger and respect. Then, as Kettleby and Elowen walked towards the wharf, Ann, Maben and Bethsany set up their stall for the day's trade.

It wasn't long before Ann realised that something was amiss. The market boy did not bring a stool for Bethsany as was usual; he had turned away in an abrupt manner upon Bethsany's call. And she could see accusing eyes in the crowd — hear certain words that were being whispered among the market traders: traitors, Roundheads, papes.

Bethsany could feel it, too. She sent Maben to find some good apples, only to see him pushed this way and that by three boys lurking near the gaol.

'What is it, sister?' said Ann. When Bethsany pointed, Ann walked over to where the bullies were standing, admonishing them for their ungodly nature. 'We're not ungodly, Mistress. 'Tis *you* who works for the devil!' they said. ''Tis you who helped Fairfax take back the castle.'

The boys slouched off before she could defend herself. Was that what they all thought? That Ann and Bethsany were in league with Parliament? That they were to blame for the castle's fall?

Throughout the morning, the sisters sat in the busy square but it soon became clear that buyers were avoiding their stall. Even when Bethsany marked down the chickens, there was no interest. It was as if a cold shadow had settled only on them while Falmouth town was bathed in light.

Ann picked up a wooden crate and set it down in the middle of the square. She made a call to prayer, a call that was invariably answered whenever Ann stood high and began her preaching. Not today. There was no gathering of the faithful; no members of her regular congregation came, eager to listen to Ann's sermon. There was only avoidance and condemnation and a sense of darkness in people's souls.

Raising her voice, Ann spoke of mercy; she spoke about loving thy neighbour; about the act of caring for neighbours who find themselves in distress. And she spoke of the devil, how he burrows deep into men's brains, twisting their logic until they mistake violence for righteousness; how they fall under the devil's spell and commit the foulest atrocities in the name of the Lord. She said all these things; and yet the people in the crowded marketplace ignored her.

Ann climbed down and made her way to Bethsany. Nothing had been sold.

'Let us go home, sister. We will eat well this evening with a rich chicken broth and distribute the rest to our neighbours.'

Maben helped Bethsany and Ann clear the stall. They walked across the square, the market day crowd parting in their wake, and made their way up the hill towards the tree-lined entrance at the crest, through which they made the steep climb that took them to the open grassland and the sparkling stream that ran parallel to the forest. It was as they walked along the trackway that they were met by the smell of smoke – black, acrid smoke that drifted from their dwelling, and which Ann immediately identified as work done by the devil's hand.

(iv)

The small thatched roofed cottage was a billowing furnace. Outside, the chicken coop had been torn down, the animals done for by a sharp blade. Further along the trackway they saw more smoke – Elowen's grandmother's dwelling had suffered the same fate. Maben, confused and scared, began to scream in that manner of his whenever violence occurred. Bethsany took good hold of him, held the child tight against her apron. There was nothing that could be done – the heat generated from within made it impossible to draw close and attack the flames with water.

'Where is Gallant?' Ann said. She looked towards the forest and began to shout: 'Gallant! Gallant!' As she did so, she saw more smoke rising above the tall trees at the far side, the side of the forest where Elijah's dwelling stood.

While Bethsany tended Maben, Ann walked towards Elowen's grandmother's dwelling. The form of an animal came into view and her heart began to pound. At first, she wasn't sure if Gallant was lying on his side sleeping, in that way of his, near to his home. But it soon became clear that he was dead. Ann knelt beside the old hound's body, his teeth bared, his eyes glazed and soulless. She closed her eyes and said a silent prayer, stroked the smooth grey fur of his head. Ann's sadness began to seep away, turning quickly to anger and defiance.

(v)

It was late afternoon when the gangplank was pulled away from the *Adventurer*. The bright morning had cooled and dark clouds were drifting over Falmouth harbour. Dan Arent walked along the deck, overseeing the new crew members as they lashed the sails and leaned over the prow in search of any hindrance to the ship's progress. The paying passengers shouted to friends and onlookers who had gathered on the wharf. Cadwaller, ready at the wheel, was informing Kettleby and Elowen of their jobs. Arent looked down at the few Parliamentary troops who were observing proceedings. He gave the order to a group of local fishermen to untie the securing ropes and hurl them on deck.

The *Adventurer* drifted slowly from the wharf. Cadwaller yelled for the jib to be unfurled. At the prow, Kettleby watched the ship's easy progress; smaller boats worked hard either side to keep the *Adventurer* steady and not allow her to drift too far. As the ship settled, ready to cut her course, Cadwaller called a sudden about turn, demanding that the

Adventurer return to the wharf.

'What in God's name are you doing, Cadwaller?' Arent yelled. There was confusion as the oarsmen in the smaller boats began to drill deep and push the ship port side. Kettleby threw the ropes to the fishermen and, running each rope through one of the wharf's iron cleats, they heaved into a pull and drew the old ship back. As he scoured the wharf to see why Cadwaller had put a halt to their disembarkation, Arent saw three figures waiting to board: Ann, Bethsany and Maben.

(vi)

A while passed before the gangway was secured and Ann made her way along. Arent took hold of her hand and kissed it, as was his nature.

'So, you have thought more on it,' he said.

Ann nodded. 'God speaks in many ways, Captain. He spoke to me this morning in a commanding voice.'

Arent smiled. 'Then my faith in Him is close to being restored, Mistress.'

Kettleby and Elowen helped Bethsany and Maben on board. The fishermen who held fast the ropes hurled them once again onto the ship's deck. Cadwaller gave the order: the *Adventurer* was ready to make sail for a second time.

The crowd lining the wharf watched and waved as the ship sailed to the mouth of Falmouth harbour. Then they turned away to go about their daily business, whether it was in the market square or in the fish huts or in some other capacity that benefited the town.

Atop the castle's turret, a raggedy girl watched too, from behind one of the crenelations, as the *Adventurer* finally pulled away in the direction of the channel. She saw figures on deck gazing at Pendennis, the great sentinel that looked out over a wide expanse of sea. But the figures were too distant for her to recognise. Had she been able to, she would have realised that Ann, Bethsany and her twin brother were among those intent on a silent, final farewell. And they in turn did not spy the girl, or notice lurking in the shadows amongst the trees below, a figure in black sitting on a smoothed stone in front of a fire. And other things were happening on board known only to those involved. Cadwaller made his way to the captain's quarters and unfurled from a blanket a small hoard of treasure that he had "rescued" from the Prince of Wales's chest, enough to set all their lives on a comfortable path for many years to come. This act brought much laughter from Arent and his deputy as the ship tacked due east and the wind filled her sails. And Kettleby and Elowen, alone together at the prow, stole a kiss and declared their everlasting love. Eventually the passengers and crew began to focus on the task and journey in hand and thought nothing more of all the strange and disturbing things they had recently witnessed.

End

Author's Note

The siege of Pendennis Castle lasted from March to August, 1646. This fictional re-telling features characters from recorded history as well as characters plucked from imagination. General Fairfax, Sir John Arundell, Richard Arundell, The Prince of Wales (later Charles II), and Sir Paul Pindar all played a role in the English Civil Wars, either in Cornwall or beyond. Elowen, Ann Netherton, Bethsany, Dan Arent, Cadwaller Jones and Maben are imaginary creations.

There is evidence that certain events in the narrative took place, most notably the shelling of the castle by Parliamentary forces, and the capture of a vessel attempting to drop supplies to the Pendennis garrison. Other events, such as the scuttling of the Prince of Wales's horse-drawn carriage and the assassination attempt before he boarded the *Phoenix*, are not, to my knowledge, recorded.

Throughout the novel I have remained, in my mind's eye, broadly faithful to the existing layout of Falmouth town (and which certainly does not correlate with the period.) For example, the steep road that Fairfax descends, leading to the market square, corresponds to today's Killigrew Street. The fictional tavern that Dan Arent and Ann Netherton visit lies in the vicinity of high street, near the town centre car park. And, although there is no evidence of a church existing before 1662, I have sited a small place of worship where the Church of King Charles the Martyr now stands. Arwenack

House still exists, though in the form of residential apartments. Remnants of the seventeenth century building can be seen from the road. Finally, the imaginary realm high above town where Ann, Elowen and Bethsany live lies beyond the traffic island at the top of Killigrew Street.

My intention with this novel was to capture the spirit of the time and bring to life a little-known chapter of the English civil wars. More importantly, though, was a desire to discover the story that existed within the history.

Acknowledgements

Thanks to: everyone at Kindle Book Publishing for their first-rate editing and formatting of my manuscript.

To: Steve Bartrick (ancestryimages.com) for permission to use "Pendennis Castle, in Cornwall" as the cover art for this book.

To: the creative writing site Abc Tales.com

My go-to reference book during research for this novel was *Cornwall in the Great Civil War and Interregnum 1642-1660* by Mary Coate (Clarendon Press, 1933).

Pendennis Castle is administered by English Heritage. It is open to the public throughout the year.

About the author

Mark Kilburn was born in Birmingham. From 1996 - 98 he was writer in residence at the City Open Theatre, Arhus, Denmark. In 2002, he was awarded a Canongate prize for new fiction and in 2020 he was placed first in the Cerasus Poetry Olympics competition. His debut novel, *Hawk Island*, was originally published by electronpress (currently out of print). His poetry collection, *Beautiful Fish*, is available from Amazon (paper) and Cerasus Poetry (digital).